SOLO DANCING

Bringing Boldness to Life

Rachel Grotheer

Contents

Introduction

I n recent years, I have become more drawn to reading nonfiction, because surprisingly, the stories are better. Many memoirs have taught me that real stories, the ones people have actually lived, are filled with more significance, spontaneity, romance, and courage than what we create for ourselves in the land of fiction. Fictional stories may have more interesting settings and happier endings, but you can't beat the character development of real people.

While I am only 24, I have a handful of big, eventful stories I love to share. I know I can't be the only one who has great stories, so I reasoned I must not be asking my friends the right questions to unearth all of theirs! I want to ask more interesting and more detailed questions to discover more about the people in my life than simple, everyday conversation reveals.

The biggest question I've started to ask is: **"When have you felt the boldest in your life?"** So far, it has seemed to stump most people.

Why am I so hung up on the word 'bold'? It's a little word with big impact. To me, boldness involves a mixture of confidence and courage, and it means overcoming fears and taking risks decisively. Being bold is very different from being naive.

Unfortunately, when we are naive and are unable to see the risks we take, we often have to stumble through the consequences.

Business professionals often talk about the value of being bold and taking risks in the workplace. Some companies even include 'bold' in their list of core company values. But it's an adjective people don't use often enough when we move out of the career world and into our personal lives. To be honest, I never thought about what it meant to be bold until someone told me that I was. They gave me examples of decisions I had made in the short time we knew each other, and showed me I had, in fact, often been bold. This was a conversation that transformed how I view myself, my goals, and the way I want to live my life; it has emboldened me to continue to 'go for it!'

I hope to do the same by pointing out moments I have recognized boldness in others, even when they don't see it in themselves. Hopefully, speaking about it with them will help them see themselves in a more positive light as well.

In this book, I have compiled stories from some people I feel very fortunate and proud to have known. I have sat down and had conversations with them, asking them to share stories of times when they felt bold. Everyone I've asked, including myself, had to think deeply about the question to understand what boldness meant to them, and even more intentionally to determine what they felt was their boldest moment.

With any bold action comes a certain level of risk, and risks don't always pay off in the way we hoped or expected. Sometimes, the only reward is a lesson learned. I have asked those in this book to consider the long-term impacts of their 'bold moment,' in hopes of providing more color to the risk vs. reward payoff.

You will see there are different ways in which people can be bold. There can be bold questions, bold choices, bold actions, and bold statements. My friends have shared stories about romance, adventure, family, career, and then some. Hopefully, reading these stories of everyday boldness will spark a train of thought leading you to recognize boldness in your own life, and encourage you to challenge yourself to aspire to be bold, or continue to be bold, whichever applies to you.

Where It All Started

My first interview with my mom is what got me really excited to get this whole thing started. I hope and pray as I continue to ask even more people for their 'bold moment,' that the conversation goes as well as this one. Alright, so it wasn't just one conversation, it was several, over a few weeks. But that's my point—I hope this isn't just one conversation, but instead, the dialogue on boldness lingers and empowers you moving forward.

I knew my mom would not initially call herself or her actions bold. Don't misunderstand me, I think she has been bold, but I was quite sure she would not think of herself in that way. This is because her boldness isn't glaringly obvious to an outsider. My mom is a tax accountant, still working for the same team, within the same company she has been with throughout my entire life. Her time outside work is best enjoyed laying on the couch reading a romance novel while a Doctor Who rerun plays in the background. When she looks at her everyday life compared to some of the exciting opportunities I have had recently, she would never think my definition of bold would include her. She would think the boldness I am referring to only shows up in stories with physical danger.

I sat down beforehand and thought of specific moments I deemed perfect examples of boldness in her life. Three or four ideas came almost immediately, and I was so excited to share them with her. I started the conversation while we were on a seven-minute drive to visit family friends. I am aware seven minutes is hardly the ideal amount of time for a long-winded talker like me to have a deep conversation with my mom, hoping it might change how she perceives herself. No, I could have picked a better setting for that particular discussion, to be sure, but in those seven minutes, which can probably be best described as me talking quickly, trying to give intentional eye contact while keeping my eyes safely on the road, I planted the first seed. The conversation shifted once we had company, but I could tell she wouldn't forget what we had discussed.

Pretty soon the ideas began to flow, and this time my mom was the source. We went on a walk, which many of my friends would say is extremely "on brand" for me. Since I no longer live at home, one of my favorite activities to do when I visit is to take a walk with my mom. She lets me talk about whatever is on my mind, and always asks questions, which gives me the opportunity to spend even more time talking about myself. During this walk, however, I was intentional about doing more of the asking and listening. She shared a couple ideas on the walk, but what happened afterwards was my absolute favorite part. We were both working from home throughout the week, but were on separate floors so I wouldn't disturb her while talking on the phone. We would see each other briefly when I came up for a snack, dance party, or to pet the dogs. In those brief moments she would say, "Oh—I thought of another one!" and give me another 'bold moment.' She would come down to my space in the basement and say, "Do you have a second? I got another one!"

This is what the entire exercise is about. Even though my mom is someone I have known my entire life, I was now asking her a question I had never asked her before. That question, "when is a time where you felt bold?" gave me many stories. Some of them I had heard multiple times, but many were new. Even after 24 years of knowing someone, you can still learn so much more. As you can see, in just the first week, she was able to think of more and more examples where she felt bold, and I hope it continues. I hope she continues to remember more bold moments, but also hope she will continue to create them, especially now since she recognizes she has that capability within her.

Now, I know I have told you my mom came up with several bold stories to share, but I am going to share just one. It takes place in the summer of 1992, when my mom, Christine— Chris for short—had just graduated from the Masters of Accounting program at UNC Chapel Hill. She had spent most of her social time in high school and college enjoying the friendship of either one or two best friends at a time and had been in a couple long term relationships. She didn't hang out in large groups, opting to have meaningful relationships with a select few. One minor exception to this tendency was when a handful of classmates would regularly grab dinner after their corporate accounting class.

So, when Chris' best friends moved away from Chapel Hill following graduation, she found herself in a challenging predicament. She loved fireworks and was excited to watch the Fourth of July celebration in Raleigh, assuming the capital would be putting on quite the show. But she didn't want to go alone. She didn't know many people in town, but one of the guys from her dinner group was still there. He had recently included her when his roommates had a celebration, where she remembered him saying a blessing before they had dinner. 'Wow, he's a Christian, too,' she might have thought. Plus, she felt comfortable around him because he never tried to hit on her. So, she decided to ask this guy whom she didn't really know, but had a couple things in common with, if he might want to go watch the fireworks with her. This was not an easy decision for her, as she did not really know him. She didn't know if he would want to go with her, and she had never called someone out of the blue to initiate a friendship.

She picked up the phone. She put it back down. She did it again. Probably another time for good measure! Then, she picked up the phone and placed the call. She asked if he would be willing to watch the Raleigh Fourth of July fireworks with her, and much to her relief, he said yes! During the conversation, they realized they were both free right at that moment. So, he came over to swim and they ordered pizza from Domino's. A couple days later, they watched the fireworks, and continued hanging out in the days to come. They enjoyed each other's company, and eventually became more than just friends. That's right, you guessed it, this is the story of how my parents started dating! Now, every year on their anniversary, even if someone can't get out of a late night of work, they share a black olive pizza from Domino's, and I think it's the cutest thing ever!

Looking back, my mom says, "I put myself out there, called someone I really didn't know, and asked if they wanted to hang out with me. But I did it, I made the call." By making the call, even though she says she "doesn't usually initiate calling people," she kickstarted the most important relationship of her life, eventually having two children together. Talk about a risk paying off well, at least in my obviously biased opinion!

After talking to my mom about her boldness, I focused on my dad.

Committed to Fairness

Duane Grotheer is much more than the man listed as my emergency contact. I am very thankful to have a father who means so many things to me, and I am proud to share him with you. My dad, like many great parents, works hard to give me a life filled with more opportunities and comfort beyond what he experienced growing up. He kept food on the table, and when he had time, he also cooked it for us. When I envision my dad in our kitchen, he's getting really excited about some new healthy recipe that gives him an excuse to use one of his many, many cast-iron pots or pans.

There are plenty of words I can use to describe my dad, including bold, but another that comes to the top of my mind is 'committed.' My entire life, it has been clear where my dad's commitments are, and he has shown it in his words, actions, and time. He is 100% committed to our family. He committed so much of his time and energy towards volunteering with our church youth group as a way to spend more time with me. There, he was given the nickname 'Stache' during a dodgeball tournament and reveled in the name proudly for years to come, waxing his mustache so it would curl. He was arguably even more committed towards being the Scoutmaster of my brother's troop, spending many weekends at campouts. He is committed to his marriage with my mom and for as long as I can remember, he has been committed to clearly telling me how much he loves and is proud of me.

He is committed to his work, and like any good accountant, he was committed to teaching me how to save my money instead of spending it. He asked me to keep track of every penny I spent as a child. He verified my receipts and journal with me, and he would match my investments into the bank. He wants me to be confident in my decisions, and will help me think out loud, but in the end, he will say, "you're an adult, and you can ask for my opinion, but you don't need my permission." I don't know if this was his intention all along, but even with this freedom, I made the same decisions he did. I ran cross country in high school like he did, though not nearly as fast, and attended his alma mater,

UNC Chapel Hill. I proclaimed faith in the same God, and became an official member of the church where he and my mom got married.

I chose to include my dad in this book, because I knew he would be supportive, as he always is. He plays such a big part in who I am today, and why I feel emboldened in many of my choices. This book would not be complete without some Duane in it!

On his own, my dad sees himself as a rule follower, and in his words, "I just keep my head down and do what's expected of me." I see this to be true in some sense; he works hard and often it turns into very long hours in the office. Many times, in recent years, he would just come home and to go to bed, then get up the next day and do the same thing all over again. The man doesn't take his vacation time either.

I tell you all this because when I asked my dad about when he had been bold, his gut reaction was that he had not been. He doesn't have much time for hobbies and doesn't often find himself in any physical danger. But I wasn't looking for a story of danger; I was looking for a story that told me more about him. I sat with him and shared a few examples of when I thought his actions were above and beyond. To these, he shrugged, saying they were simply, "solid choices, more than anything else." He didn't feel like he had a choice for most of these instances. To me, it sounded like he just made his choices instantly. For things he considers no-brainers, like a sense of family obligation or doing the next right thing, his mind is made up before the question is asked.

At this point, I asked, "have your priorities and values ever been in jeopardy? Have you ever needed to stand up for something or someone?" To this, he immediately answered, "Oh certainly," as if this was something everyone goes through regularly. He gave me a scenario at work where he noticed something he didn't consider to be fair. "If I see something that's unfair, I can't sit by and let it continue," he said, explaining why he found his next choice obvious. With little to no hesitation, he raised the issue to the attention of his company's President and COO. He met with them repeatedly, until the situation was resolved. Raising an issue like this, to the highest in command, undoubtedly put his job on the line. If they disagreed or didn't appreciate his choice of words when he was fired up and passionate, he could be finished. Duane knew all these things, but his values simply took priority. After several, and sometimes heated discussions, the unfair situation was resolved. With the workplace feeling repaired, his sense of guilt and discomfort disappeared.

His decision process here was brief and lacked plot twists. It didn't drastically change his life. They didn't fire him, nor did he immediately get promoted after they realized his strong moral character. Big details or events like those hypotheticals are not what makes bold stories 'great' in my eyes. It is the acknowledgement of risk and choosing what is right over the easy or expected path. It's the growth and the humanness of this story that draws me to it – the character development I crave, but don't always get through my fictional readings.

He would step up again if he felt his voice was needed, I am sure of it. I am also equally sure, like my dad, many others don't see some of their regular decisions for what they truly are - bold. I encourage you to ask yourself the same questions here. Have you ever stood up for something you believed in? Do you think there could be something you might refer to as normal, but it is a big deal? I would be willing to bet there is.

1

Basics of Boldness

I will share many examples of myself, friends, and family in our boldest moments. The purpose of sharing these stories with you is to show you how boldness can be wrapped up in many ways. Reading these examples, themes, and patterns of boldness, will help you to recognize and remember your own boldness.

It is crucial to include stories from multiple people, because boldness can look different for each person. When our fears and faiths differ, so do our examples of boldness. Just because a choice is bold for your friend doesn't mean it's bold for you and vice versa. If you fear standing out from the crowd, dancing by yourself at a concert could be out of your comfort zone, but to another who fears missing out, it may be scarier to stay home from the concert and focus on a different task. If I have always struggled with a fear of commitment and you have always struggled with a fear of abandonment, boldness in relationships may look very different for us. Faith can differ among individuals, too. For example, someone may have faith that when they fail, their closest friends and family will be there to support them.

Others may have faith that despite their mistakes, God's plan for their life will still come to fruition. Another source of hope could be in one's self, that they would be strong enough to handle what's coming next. Having faith in someone or something can give you the confidence to take risks.

Because of these discrepancies in faith and fear, our comfort zones look different from one another, making it hard for our boldness to be recognizable. You may not know if someone is stepping outside of their comfort zone unless you ask. Our boldness is not always obvious or public; sometimes, it's a little more hidden. Other times, boldness happens behind closed doors - just like the best solo dance parties. Just because you don't see it happening, doesn't mean there is no dancing going on. For this reason, I will include stories from many people who may not have appeared bold to those who witnessed their experience.

I am surrounded by arguably the best and boldest people in the world, and I can't wait to prove it to you. For a while, I attributed many of these great friendships to myself. I was prideful and thought I was the link who connected groups who wouldn't otherwise spend time together. I also believed I had the best friends around me because I had extremely good taste in friends and was a great judge of character. But in the end, it is not about me.

It took a global pandemic for me to realize that truth. I moved across the country from Chicago to Orange County, California on March 11, 2020. This was the precise time period when toilet paper was a hot commodity. My roommate and I went to five different stores in one day, and finally begged a stranger at Staples to give us one of the packs she had gleaned from the shelves. With severe lockdown measures and curfews, this was a challenging time to make new friends. Yet within a couple months, I was part of a group of six women who became just that - true friends. This was the first time when I could not reason my perceived friendship skills as the 'glue' to the group. We met through a virtual Bible study, and eventually shifted from one-off walks and picnics to a long weekend in Mammoth. Our weekend trip made the differences among the women clear. Our ages ranged from 22 to 29; our chosen careers included acting, engineering, and marketing. Even with interests, the only thing we had in common throughout the group was our gender and our faith. This weekend helped me reevaluate, understanding my friends were not perfectly secured by my own doing, but placed into my life by God.

Don't be surprised when I name-drop God in my stories. He is a big part of who I am and what has happened to me, so I am giving recognition where it is due. I don't expect all my readers to have similar beliefs to me, but this context is important in sharing my personal story. For example, trusting God for Christian community and financial security has given me the freedom to take risks. I feel emboldened by my faith as I take risks like moving across the country three times in two years for work; it will all end up for the best. I am confident the Lord's plan is superior to my own, and this gives me hope in what is to come, even when I don't know what will happen next. Perhaps your confidence in 'everything will work out fine' comes from something else and is what emboldens you to try new things.

I hope to show following God creates opportunity for boldness, but also asks I boldly become more like Him. This can come out in many ways; one example might be to risk not having anything to contribute to a conversation should I refuse to gossip. It can be so much easier or natural to join in, and it takes boldness to choose to refrain. I hope whatever your personal beliefs and motivations are, you will see there is room for boldness as you live them out.

I have asked everyone to be open and vulnerable with me during our discussions, and in their decision to let me share their story. It only seems fitting I am equally as vulnerable when sharing my own stories. I typically consider myself an open book, but you will get a direct lens into some of the most challenging parts of my life. I have my share of cheerful stories, but that is hardly the whole picture. Several of my bold moments were painful, even excruciating, but they have shaped me into who I am today. Other stories are examples of my ignorance or naivety - they were not bold, because I truly believed there was no risk being taken. I hope to show the difference through the stories I share and pray I will have more common sense going forward, so the stories will be more likely bold, than naïve or reckless. I will kickstart this book with my favorite bold story of my own!

So many people have taken a trip to Europe after graduating that it has become almost stereotypical. I don't typically think of myself as 'mainstream' or 'basic,' but I was certainly excited about my turn at this popular vacation idea. I planned a trip with some of my best friends from school; we were going to hit several different countries over a span of 2-3 weeks. But as the spring semester continued, they started to drop out of the trip, one by one. By the time I was looking to book my flight, I didn't have anyone left who could join me for this European adventure. But my mind was set. I had saved the money, and once I started my job in July, I didn't know when the next opportunity for a long vacation like this would come along again. I talked to my parents about what I should do. We agreed, it didn't feel safe for me to go alone. I wracked my brain, desperately attempting to think of anyone who might be able to join me.

Eventually, I remembered a future coworker of mine, who I'll call Chase, was going on his own European trip. The reason it took me so long to think of Chase was I hardly knew him. We met at a work event, spending a couple hours together in a group. For our rotational program at work, we were to move locations every eight months for a total of two years. Chase and I were both assigned to spend our first rotation in Chicago. We were the only ones from the group looking to have a roommate there, so we had texted about the possibility of living together.

Seemingly out of the blue, I texted Chase a very specific question. "Are you still going to be in Europe May 26 - June 10?" He replied that yes, he and a couple of his best friends from college were going to be there then, and a couple weeks before that, too. Next, I texted Chase a very bold question. "Can I join you?" Some people feel guilty about inviting themselves over to a house party or dinner, and here I was, inviting myself to a two-week trip in foreign countries, with people I didn't even know! This was Chase's last chance to spend quality time with his best friends before they moved away from each other; why would he want a random girl inserting herself into those memories and pictures? My presence would interrupt their originally scheduled 'bro time.' Despite this, Chase took a chance on me, saying yes, and added me to their plans.

I flew into Europe through Paris, spending one night in a hotel by myself. My solo day in Paris felt like a movie, but brings up an example of a very naïve me. I had just got myself a crepe, when I walked by a man in front of a rickshaw bike. He asked me a question, I can't remember what, and I answered him. He was so happy I answered him, instead of ignoring him like everyone else, he felt compelled to thank me. He then said, "Would you like a ride around the corner to the Louvre? No charge. I'm done for the day, so I need to drop it back off over there anyway." I asked, "You sure?" and then I got in.

Once we were on the road, he asked, "do you have time? I can show you around the rich part of Paris on the way, I think you'll like it." I agreed and texted a friend back home what was going on, as if somehow my friend would be able to keep me safe if this man ended up kidnapping me or dropping me off in a section of town where I would surely be lost.

He ended up taking me on a 3-hour tour, hopping out periodically to show me sights and take my picture. We went to Le Marias, where he stopped in the middle of the road in front of a crowded restaurant and hollered. The owner came out, kissed both my cheeks, and handed me a free falafel. I know it wasn't Rome, but I sure felt like somehow, I was Lizzie McGuire in her movie. We also stopped at an art gallery, where the owner gave me a quick tour of the art on display. Then we passed by a bar, and he asked if I would like to join him for drinks. It was now getting dark, and this is finally when my common sense kicked in. I said, "no, I have a train to catch, can you drop me back off at the Louvre?" He did, and I said thanks before speed-walking my butt back to the hotel.

The next morning, I caught a train to meet Chase and his friends in Montpellier, France. We spent time exploring the shops and network of alleyways, getting to know each other. After Montpellier, we went further west to Bordeaux, studying about red wine. Chase and I came back from dinner one night and spontaneously decided we were ready to leave for the next leg of the trip. We booked flights for the next morning to Mykonos, Greece, without plans of where to stay once we arrived. The two of us split off from his friends before sunrise the next morning, leaving in a rush of excitement. This would be our platonic 'roomie honeymoon.'

Fortunately, we found a last second spot in a cheap hostel and made friends with travelers our age. Emboldened by the presence of three new female travelers, I proclaimed to the girls if I was ever going to skinny dip, it would be here in Greece. The four of us scoped out one of the beaches at night, but there were bouncers guarding the waters. They didn't want anyone coming from the clubs and drowning, so night time looked like a no-go.

The next day, we walked around the island in daylight, realizing one of the beaches was a nude beach. I did not think I was ready for something quite that public, but now we at least had an idea.

The next morning, while our group of new friends were at a beach in front of the hostel, the little band of girls got up, and I asked Chase if he could watch our stuff. Without giving him any other context, we walked 20 minutes to the other side of the island and found a semi-private dock next to the nude beach. We got in the clearest water I had ever been in, and a minute later we had all thrown our bathing suits up onto the dock. It was about 11am, a clear sunny day, and my pale skin was surely blinding someone walking on a distant trail. Bold! I expected it to be exhilarating or exciting, but honestly it was simply relaxing. I felt indescribably free!

To understand the significance of that moment, I am briefly changing the subject to my relationship with food. Don't worry, we will get back to Greece soon.

My last year of school, I hated my body. My self-image first became negative after a summer where I had gained ten pounds. I entered my senior year approaching my diet and exercise with a vengeance. As many young women understand, the focus on being healthy can quickly change to an unhealthy bodily fixation. Every single time I passed a mirror, I would lift my shirt to check the progress of my stomach, sucking it in, unsatisfied. I did cleanses and went through periods where I would exercise at least three times a day, but I still didn't like myself compared to the rest of the girls on the club cross country team. I started skipping meals, strategically picking ones where no one would notice. If my roommates were not in the kitchen, I would skip breakfast. I would bring salads when I had lunch plans with friends, and skip dinner while I ran from one activity to the next. It took months for any change, but suddenly in a span of three weeks, I returned to my previous weight.

This is the only thing in my life I haven't shared with others. Typically, I overshare, but this particular battle, I decided to keep private.

By the end of the school year, I was neither proud of my body, nor my actions to enforce change upon it. I started to seek out truths. One helpful choice was to attend a body image course through my campus ministry after graduation. I learned God needs diversity of beauty to accurately depict His glory and His creation. I had been limiting the definition of beauty by thinking it only applied to the skinny girls I saw around me. Another empowering lesson was on the intentional purpose of food in scripture: used as an act of His provision, an element of hospitality, community, and sacraments. As these bits of wisdom sank in, I slowly, but surely, stopped skipping meals over the following year. I still lift my shirt to check my stomach most of the time when passing mirrors, but I spend less time worrying about calories consumed, and instead focus on adding nutrients.

This act of swimming was the first moment of peace with my body I had in a long time. By no means did this act of swimming freely change everything, but it was liberating. I am surprised by God's use of skinny dipping to help me love another part of His creation: me!

In Greece, our little pack of girls was interrupted by someone asking if they could take a picture with us. To this, we quickly and firmly said no. Time to suit back up. We came back to Chase and the other guys we knew, whom we had abandoned for over an hour and a half. That day felt pretty darn bold to me, facing my insecurities, and checking something off the bucket list.

That afternoon, my boldness and spontaneity continued with another new experience. I hopped on the back of an ATV with a guy I had met briefly at the hostel, another girl doing likewise. We decided to explore the island, and as we reached the furthest point from the hostel, one of the other ATV's gaslights started blinking. We didn't know how much was left, so we needed to take the most direct route possible.

One thing you should know about me - I am horrible with navigation. One time I was on my way from Chapel Hill, NC to Charlotte, NC and found myself in Virginia. Yet, here I was, the only one with cell data to navigate us to a gas station. On the ATV's, I couldn't get my driver's attention in time for a turn, so we missed it. Finally, he understood what I was yelling, and he stopped. To our dismay, the ATV with the low gas light flew past us, continuing in the wrong direction. We darted back after them, honking our horn. He thought we were messing around, so he just honked back. Agh! Eventually, we got him to turn back in the direction of the gas station. Just before we arrived, we approached a long line before a roundabout. He gunned it, passing the rest of the line and going the wrong direction around the roundabout to get to the gas station ASAP. I held my breath, watching until they made it through. They arrived at the gas station before running out. Not much longer, we made it back to the hostel, and I felt a record level of spontaneity in the actions of my previous week.

A few days later, Chase and I rejoined his group in Barcelona, then I split off again to fly back home through Paris. My big risk of traveling abroad with a group of practically strangers, ended up being an absolute blast. I felt the reality of God's provision as I safely returned home, with another friend carefully placed in my life. I hadn't known Chase beforehand, but we knew each other well afterwards. We separated for three weeks before reuniting as roommates in Chicago. The trip made it so I was even more excited about what the experience in Chicago would be, because now I had a good friend going through it all with me.

This bold question changed my life in more ways than one, many of them unexpected. Perhaps the most unexpected thing of all is that Chase said yes, and let me join. I anticipated a no, like I had heard from many friends in the weeks before. If he had said no, I would have tried my best to find another way to travel, but it would have turned out much differently, I'm sure.

What is the boldest question you have asked someone? What would you ask if you were not afraid of a "no" answer?

A Famous Example

It feels necessary to dive into a short and memorable story now. It involves a friend, who we'll call Rico, who made me feel welcome in my early days at college. After graduation, we parted ways, only later reconnecting when we both lived in Charlotte. He was quickly excited by my question of boldness in his life, and we ended up talking for four hours. It felt like we were addressing some of the world's biggest problems by asking this one new question. As we talked about what boldness meant, and why it was important, he came up with a couple stories.

Those who know me well, know that every strong emotion I have produces tears, but most commonly while I am laughing. No doubt about it, this story had me crying and laughing.

Rico took a freshman seminar class, and on the first day, his professor asked each student to answer a philosophical question, "why do people tell the truth?" As he went down the row, everyone answered something along the lines of "it's the golden rule," "it's the right thing to do," and so on. Rico could sense these answers were not satisfying the professor, so when it was his turn, he said, "so they can lie more effectively." His professor exclaimed "YES! Exactly!" and took a special interest in Rico from that point on. At the end of the semester, he revealed to Rico he was the summer intern advisor for the White House and offered Rico an opportunity to work there with him.

In Rico's first week of the internship, he found himself in a room, surrounded by other summer staffers and his advisor.

They were all waiting patiently for a meeting with the Vice President at the time. One can expect the Vice President of the United States has a packed agenda, going from one meeting to the next throughout the day. So, it was no surprise that he was running 15-20 minutes late.

The Vice President came in the door and hurriedly sat down, apologizing for his tardiness. Rico sarcastically responded for the group, "Yeah that was SOOO rude of you!" The other interns turned and stared at him wide eyed, clearly shocked. He could feel his advisor giving him the death glare, and he immediately regretted his bold joke. In his uncomfortable and now anxious state, Rico waited to see what would come next. The Vice President doubled over, cracking up. He said, "that is the funniest thing I have ever heard! You and me, let's get lunch today!" and then he started the meeting. At his invitation, Rico and his advisor went to lunch with the Vice President that day, and he felt an amicable relationship with him the rest of the summer.

I chose to include Rico's story in part because of the memorable celebrity encounter, but also because it is indicative of one of my biggest goals through these conversations. I had known about Rico's summer in the White House, but had never heard of this encounter. It is likely it never would have felt relevant if I had not brought up my boldness project with him. I'm so glad I did.

When have you surprised those around you? When have you been true to yourself, even when you don't know your audience personally?

Stereotypically Bold

Next, I'd like to focus on an example that might align with your first impression of the word bold, because it has an element of physical danger. This example comes from one of my close friends from college, Miles. Some knew him as an extremely driven student, and if they ever saw him outside the library, they would also know him as hilariously witty. He is half of the most iconic duo I know: Matt & Miles. I tried a fun exercise with them, asking Matt what Miles' boldest moment was, which produced a story of Miles intentionally sneezing into Matt's open mouth when he saw him yawning. Gross, but hilarious, right? Surprisingly not the story Miles decided to go with. We will get back to Matt later.

Miles was one of the first people I asked, "What was a time when you felt bold?" We spent a long time debating the definition of the word bold. After I went down a long rabbit hole creating my own definition, Miles got impatient and googled it. For those of you who are more practical like Miles, the definition he found was 'showing an ability to take risks; confident and courageous.[1]' He reasoned many of his actions may appear bold to others but are results of his assertive personality. He's right; it often is hard to accurately recognize boldness in others, especially if you are unfamiliar with their comfort zones and risk tolerance. That is why I will try to capture some of that in the context I share in each story.

Miles claims to be extremely risk-averse, yet one of his frequent activities is trading individual stocks. Again, you see we all have different tolerances of risk. I argued even if he feels those risks are calculated and measured, he is still aware of the risk present and chooses to take it. He might feel more confident in the risk due to information he has researched or discussed with other finance-savvy friends, but it is still a little bold, even if it is not out of the ordinary for him.

Throughout the conversations I have had on boldness, most people indicated they don't think of themselves as bold. Many people would categorize themselves as risk-averse because they are not recklessly taking risks. Just because you are not reckless doesn't mean you are not bold. In fact, if you are reckless, that can be something entirely different from pure boldness.

Miles' chosen bold story takes place during his senior year of college when he lived in a house with 12 guys. One day, the guys decided to swim the length of Jordan Lake. They piled into a car, following the determination of one of the housemates, Henry. It is intriguing that Henry was the one motivating the group, because he, like Miles, knew how to swim, but would never be labeled 'a swimmer.' He and Miles were confident in their overall athletic ability but didn't realize what it would be like until they started. Miles had been a lifeguard in previous years, but in this scenario, he would be testing his physical limits.

Just in case, they had chosen a route close to a natural wall to provide a resting option since the water was too deep to stand. Staying true to his self-proclaimed nature, Miles kept this moment as risk-averse as he could. He was bold, not reckless.

[1] *"art, n.1." OED Online. Oxford University Press, December 2021. Web. 6 December 2021.*

They got into the choppy lake and started swimming, while their driver went to the other end and paddle-boarded out to join them part way. Miles quickly realized he couldn't breathe comfortably with the pattern of freestyle, so he switched to backstroke. The only problem with swimming backstroke was he could not tell where he was going. He decided to lift his head up and keep his eyes on a point in the distance to maintain a straight line. I don't know how strong your neck is, but that sounds exhausting to me. For the next day and a half, Miles couldn't turn his head, his neck was so sore.

Miles claims the only thing that got him through the mile of swimming was "sheer will and competitive drive." But once he got going, it got scary. He couldn't take a break by treading water, because that wouldn't be a real break. Once he was about halfway, it wouldn't make it any easier to turn back. He was exhausted, but he kept going, for fear of the alternative.

Turns out, things were not going much better for his buddy, Henry. Henry threw up in the water, but it was so deep he had to do it while treading water. He could have ended up inhaling water, choking, or worse. But since he was able to keep swimming to shore, it turned into a hilarious accident, like when someone falls down the stairs, but bounces back up again.

After all this, Miles only finished about 20 yards ahead of Henry. When the group heard about Henry's incident, they all cracked up. But they both finished successfully, and neither will be doing anything like that any time soon! This endeavor didn't turn into a lifelong passion of long-distance swimming for Miles, nor his friend Henry. In fact, Miles looks back on his experience as traumatic. But he learned how far sheer will and competitive drive could take him - approximately a mile through open water.

Some bold stories are adventurous and dangerous like Miles'. He didn't just pick a unique activity for the afternoon, but boldly faced a challenge where he was dependent on his own abilities, even though the ability was not one he had attempted before. The reason Miles' story is bold is not because of the specific action or danger. It is because he pushed the barrier of his comfort zone. For me, mimicking this attempt to swim a mile would be reckless, because I am a poor swimmer. For another friend, swimming a mile likely wouldn't be bold because he feels confident in his long-distance training in collegiate swimming. For Miles, this swim was bold, because he might be able to complete it, but he didn't know until he tried.

Just because an experience involves a near death encounter, doesn't mean it is bold. Danger can arise when risks are not anticipated or accounted for, as in the following example.

In August 2020, when I lived in Costa Mesa, CA, I went on a hike with my roommate and one of our friends. I'll refer to them as Lauren and Tina, respectively. We wanted to go to the Angeles National Forest, but our first choice of trail was closed due to a ranch fire. We chose an alternative, slightly down the road from the closed trail. We carpooled, wearing masks in the car, and noticing multiple helicopters flying overhead as we drove through the forest to the trailhead. We were trying to figure out what was going on, and Lauren made a joke that her credit card gave her medical evacuation savings.

We started our beautiful hike at Mount Waterman Loop with a leisurely pace, sharing stories and recommendations to one another. We stopped at a couple viewpoints and enjoyed our packed lunches at the summit. We restarted hiking and soon reached a trail marker. We knew if we turned to our left, it would take us back down the way we came. If we turned to our right, it looked like it would continue the 6-mile loop we saw on the map. I felt confident we should complete the loop so we would get to see more of the trail, and we all agreed. We headed significantly downhill and after a while we stopped seeing other hikers. We had the beautiful forest to ourselves. Lauren and I finished off our water, calculating we were only a few minutes away from the car. Those calculated minutes passed, and our devices tracked the completion of six miles. The problem was, we were nowhere near a road.

We had no clue where we had erred, but knew we must turn around, and in the worst case, return to the trail marker where we had previously turned. But Lauren and I were now out of water, and Tina only had a little left. Aware of Lauren's underlying health conditions, I had picked a 6-mile trail intentionally. I knew she could handle six miles, but now we had no idea how much farther we had to go. We started back-tracking up the hill and she slowed down significantly. I kept turning my head to check on her, and each time, she would smile and give me a big thumbs up. When I stopped to catch my breath and waited for her to catch up, she would say, "alright, let's keep going," without taking a break herself. I knew she must be battling a great deal of discomfort but ignored those concerns because she is a tough cookie and looked like she was hanging in there.

When we finally got a bar of cell service, we stopped to see if our online maps would load, to no avail. Then, Lauren caught up and collapsed to the ground with the words, "I can't go any further." Woah... Despite the adamance of those words, I didn't initially grasp the gravity of what was happening. I argued I could give her a piggyback ride for the rest of the way, if Tina could carry our bags. They both immediately shot my idea down, reminding me of two key points: 1) we had no idea how much farther we had to travel 2) I am not that strong. Their logic won. We would stay together as a group and call for help. Tina called 9-1-1, describing our location and outfits to the dispatcher. We were told a helicopter would be on its way, but there was no estimate as to how long it would take.

While we waited for the helicopter to arrive, we saw a hiker coming up the trail. Tina and I sprung to our feet and shouted for his attention. Fortunately, the man, let's call him Dave, was an ultramarathoner and very familiar with this neck of the woods. He went around the bend in the trail and confirmed a creek was nearby, so I went with him to fill up our water, crossing our fingers, hoping it wasn't contaminated. I reasoned Lauren was dehydrated now, and if there were bacteria or something in the water, it wouldn't be a problem until later. I gave her a full water bottle and started drinking my refilled one as well.

Dave waited with us until the helicopter came, and we ran out from the cover of the trees, waving our arms to catch its attention, but they didn't see us. The helicopter passed us and went over another peak, out of our sight. Worried, Tina called 9-1-1 again. Thankfully, the helicopter came back over the peak and slowly scanned the area. We held up our phones, attempting to reflect the sunlight off the screen. We waved our arms frantically, mine burning intensely, further proving I would have been unable to carry Lauren out of the forest myself. The helicopter moved astoundingly slow above the dispersed trees. Then finally, they saw us.

As the helicopter got closer, I still hadn't grasped the severity of the situation. In fact, my first thought was to capture this 'cool moment' on video. Until less than three seconds later, when I became afraid. The noise and winds were immense and overwhelming. I sprinted back to Lauren, who was waiting under a tree. She felt badly enough to be airlifted, and upon its arrival, she was forcibly aware of her fear of heights. The wind continued to pick up, and dirt and debris was flying everywhere. Lauren and I hit the deck, and I tried to cover her with my body. Even through my body barrier and her mask, she managed to inhale a significant amount of dirt.

While we huddled on the ground, the medic was lowered down from the helicopter by a cable. He walked over, sending the helicopter up a few hundred extra feet until he was ready. He confirmed Lauren's symptoms while he outfitted her with a helmet, goggles, and vest. He handed me her bag, taking only her phone, wallet, and inhaler into his pockets. Together he and Lauren started walking to the clearing. He signaled for the helicopter to come back towards us and drop another cable to pull them up. He yelled, "I'm taking her to Pomona Valley Hospital." I repeated the hospital name to myself, and at the last second, Lauren hollered, "Tell my mom!"

As the helicopter lowered this time, the winds were even more intense. I found myself on the ground spooning with Tina, covering our heads from the flying pinecones and brush. My hat fell off my head and my water bottle fell out of my backpack pocket. My keys fell out of my pocket too, but thankfully Tina caught them. She turned to me and yelled over the noise, "we need to leave, this isn't safe!" I responded "Where?! I can't keep my eyes open; let's stay." It felt like an eternity, laying on the ground, convinced I would somehow die. I'm embarrassed to admit this, but in my fear, I was also angry. Covering my head for safety, I didn't get to see what it looked like for Lauren to be airlifted. I was there throughout the entire experience but had no visual memory or proof.

Eventually, the helicopter flew away, giving us a chance to get our bearings. I retrieved my hat and water bottle from further down the trail. We found Dave, who to our surprise, had kept standing throughout the entire ordeal. His hat and glasses fell off, but he didn't budge. He was intent on capturing it all on video. What a legend, Dave. I was shocked, but also relieved. We would know what it looked like and we had proof!

We confirmed we had all heard the same thing minutes before: Pomona Valley Hospital. I then called Lauren's boyfriend, our third roommate at the time, and left potentially the scariest voicemail of all time. "It's Rachel! Lauren just got airlifted out of Angeles National Forest! We were hiking, got lost, ran out of water, and she got altitude sickness. They are taking her to Pomona Valley Hospital. Can you tell her parents? Oh, you won't be able to call me back, because we won't have service. Bye!"

We had five more miles to go for the remainder of our hike. There is no way I could have carried Lauren, or anyone, that far. I ended up drinking 60 ounces of that unfiltered water in total. We made it back to my car and dropped Dave off at his car a couple miles away. From there, we had another 30 minutes of driving until we regained consistent cell service. We stopped at the first gas station, where we bought clean water, and responded to a voicemail from Lauren's mom, who had gotten the message. We drove an additional 30 minutes to the hospital and waited in the parking lot for about 25 minutes until Lauren was discharged and in the car.

On the way home and once we arrived safe and sound, we laughed about how crazy it all was. We already thought our last several months were worthy of a reality TV show, which we jokingly called "Pandemic in Paradise." This would be the best season finale, we joked. We were filthy from lying in the dirt and from everything that flew at us in the winds. Relieved, exhausted, and slightly delirious, we showered and went to bed.

I have told this story countless times, and no doubt will continue to do so, because it is so absurd. This story can be described with many adjectives, but I would not call it bold. Yes, we faced and suffered from many risks. But we did not perceive those risks ahead of time. We were not bold, we were unprepared. Maybe we were a little naive. This is not an adventure I care to repeat, so now I bring a first aid kit and far more water than necessary with me on every hike.

Boldness and danger are not always intertwined. This story shows danger does not directly result from boldness. Plus, there are plenty of bold acts that can take place without ever facing physical risks. As I hope to prove through the many bold stories in this book, emotional risks can expand your comfort zone just as physical risks do.

Making a Habit of Boldness

Oskar is both hilarious and intimidating, a combo that makes him one of my favorite mentors. We bonded over UNC basketball at a work happy hour, and we have met regularly ever since. In our meetings, he has challenged me to give my own presentation of the company's quarterly earnings, but this is so outside my wheelhouse that at first, I thought he was joking! He has also assigned me books to read, then asking me multiple choice questions to understand my takeaways. With his intensity it is surprising he never fails to greet me with, "Hi, my friend! It's great to see you!" In another comical juxtaposition, Oskar oversees

Enterprise Risk, but is the biggest advocate for boldness I know. Oskar has helped me process events and decisions aloud, whether work related or personal, so it was a natural transition to bring him into my writing process.

Oskar shared when he is facing a decision, he tries to take the option that will be more challenging. He is not looking to make things inefficient, but he does intentionally seek discomfort. It doesn't sound intuitive when so many of us spend our time working towards pleasure, comfort, and luxury. Sure, we may choose delayed gratification depending on the circumstance, but how many people seek discomfort in *every* decision? Why would he want that?

This mentality started when Oskar was 14. He made a choice, "setting in motion a way of thinking for me that persists today." Prior to that, he had grown up in a poor Honduran community, where numerous American missionaries came to provide support. With the influx of missionary families, a boarding school was built locally for their children. When Oskar was in first grade, his mom was eager for him to learn English, and convinced the missionaries to let him attend their school. He was the only student who was not Caucasian. Upon completion of eighth grade, his classmates planned to attend another boarding school in Oklahoma. Oskar was supposed to join them.

Days before high school in Oklahoma started, Oskar and his dad left Honduras and purchased clothes and school supplies in Texas. Suddenly, Oskar started to have second thoughts about it all, asking himself, "what am I doing here?" Moving to school in

Oklahoma meant saying goodbye to many things. Goodbye to his family and spending time with them for birthdays, holidays, and special moments. Oskar was sure to remind me this was before the creation of FaceTime and texting. International calls were not an easy option either. Goodbye to the only country he'd ever known. Goodbye to his home, his own room. Goodbye to radios and TV. Goodbye to their "maids, driver, all the hallmarks of a relatively affluent lifestyle" he had known in recent years. Hello to a job before school every morning, new rules and restrictions, and mandatory chapel.

As Oskar contemplated all this, his dad picked up on it. "My dad is the softy; he was sensing I was having trepidation." Oskar's dad gave him an out, an opportunity to go back home, saying, "you don't have to do this…it's up to you… I'll buy the ticket now; you can come home with me." At that moment, it became Oskar's choice, he could go home now, or he could stick it out and attend this school. Talking about his dad's influence on the choice, Oskar says, "He made it simple. He was not pushing me to stay; he was basically pushing me to leave." As Oskar considered his decision, he knew for certain the "easy route would be to go home… the more uncomfortable path would be to attend this boarding school." He thought about how this choice would impact his life and the futures of his younger brother and sister, who were still at home in Honduras. He anticipated whatever he chose would determine their opportunities when they reached his age. Over the rest of that evening he thought and prayed.

Boldly, Oskar chose to stay. Looking at what turned the tide back then, Oskar remembers thinking, "'I can do this. I know it will be difficult, but it will lead to something better.' I don't know I would have been able to put into words what better actually meant." He had to have faith that facing this challenge would bring him to a better future, even if he didn't know what he wanted the future to be. He wasn't leaving because he had specific goals for a career or economic prosperity. He wasn't leaving because he knew on what path this education could send him. "I wanted to face the challenge. I wanted to face the fear."

Oskar started school and moved into a dorm with communal showers where he shared a room with three other students. They also gave Oskar a job on the farm, where he milked cows twice a day, six days a week. Each morning he would wake up at 3:30 AM, bundle up in dirty clothes, and report for duty by 4 AM. He already felt like he was different from the American students, and now he smelled like farm animals, too. "How was I going to get a girlfriend like that?" In that environment, he missed the comforts of home. "The first couple months I almost regretted that decision, but I knew I would stick it out." He did stick it out. He joined the varsity soccer team and kept doing his best. He refused to let anyone underestimate him.

"Now, looking back 30+ years later, it was the right decision." Sticking it out in Oklahoma had major implications. His hunch was right; his younger siblings both followed him to school, and they all have their own families living in the US. His kids are all "reaping the benefits of those decisions." They can go to college or take advantage of countless other opportunities. If he had stayed home in Honduras for high school, he knows he would still be in Honduras today, living a hugely different life. "There's no question to me the decision was fundamental in altering the destiny of my family... I think it was the watershed moment in my life and it was a reflection of bold thinking." Oskar had the "hope and expectation it would deliver a better outcome, and I think it has." He rose to the occasion, and it opened the door for his family members to forge their paths as well.

Even now, Oskar continues to believe in himself and face his fears. That choice as a 14-year-old created boldness as a habit for the rest of his life. He chooses adventure by pursuing the unknown, regardless of the circumstance. On different days it may look like picking up a new hobby, learning a new skill, or exploring a new place. Recently, he got a scuba diving certification with his daughters, despite how uncomfortable he feels about swimming. "I like the feeling at the end that I have faced one of my fears."

When have you accepted a challenge, not knowing what the reward would be?

2

Travel Near and Far

A common thread I have found in my bold interviews is the element of travel. This aligned with my initial hunch; I expected to hear some travel stories, since people tend to remember and tell these stories often. Even the first story I shared about myself involved travel. Going somewhere new can expose travelers to new people and a different way of life, which can be both fun and uncomfortable. That discomfort and change can be rewarding when travelers commit to experiencing a new environment. The reward could be learning about themselves, their preferences, and how they want to see themselves going forward. This may be as simple as picking up a new favorite food or hobby.

The risks and rewards can be amplified during solo travel. There are potentially more dangers traveling alone, especially as a female, but this is not the only risk. Many people, especially extroverts, have not been alone for a significant period. Several friends have described the act of being alone as uncomfortable, especially after living in a scenario surrounded by family in a home or with friends at school. I feel this on a deep personal level, because in college I did everything I could to avoid being alone. I would schedule back-to-back events and say yes to every activity rather than the possibility of sitting in stillness by myself. All my hobbies involved others, and not only did I not see the point of being alone, but I was also terrified of it. Wouldn't I be bored? Wouldn't I be left out of something else that was inevitably happening on campus? Wouldn't I be sacrificing a crucial moment of my four-year experience? Wouldn't I be lonely?

While I may be more extroverted than the average person, several people have found their first venture on their own to be significant. These next few stories will all include elements of those stepping out on their own as they travel somewhere on the globe they had never been before.

The Blueberry Intern

Matt Q. is one of the smartest and most informed people I have ever met. He would never brag about it himself, but he was a Morehead-Cain scholar at UNC, which is a very prestigious accomplishment. He earned Eagle Scout, and can play seven instruments, including guitar, banjo, and mandolin. These accomplishments are impressive, but ultimately not the reason we became friends. In addition to having a big noggin' behind his glasses, he's incredibly kind, inclusive, and witty. He shares a love for Jesus, Carolina athletics, beer, and games like Codenames. He is often seen with his partner in crime, Miles, who you just read about, or his wife, Bailey.

Matt spent the summer after freshman year of college in a vastly different way than most. Instead of going back home to his parents and taking a job like landscaping or in fast food, he travelled to what was then called Swaziland. For the geographically challenged, this is in southern Africa. He didn't go through an organized study abroad option either. He went by himself, working as a ranch hand of sorts at a dairy farm and tutor for local children in Nhlangano.

He had just done a year of long-distance dating with Bailey and was now moving further from her than he ever had before. Confident in their relationship, despite communication challenges anticipated with a 6-hour time difference, they parted ways for nine more weeks.

It took at least 17 hours in the air, spread across three flights, before he arrived at Muswati Airport. His only expectation was a man was supposed to pick him up. He had no idea what the man looked like or how to contact him. None of the signs in the airport were in English, and he describes the local language, 'SiSwati', as "so obscure, you can't really even Google translate it or learn it online." I imagine him skeptically walking through the parking lot, and his ears perking when he heard his name called out. Matt says the man who picked him up became something like an uncle to him for the duration of the summer. His 'uncle' took him to the grocery store on the way to the farm, but the rest of the summer he would get to the grocery store by walking an hour each way. Unable to depend on his parents' cooking or the convenience of a campus dining hall, Matt learned how to cook.

During the day, Matt would do various horticultural tasks on the dairy farm. He had never worked on a farm before and contrary to what he expected at a dairy farm, he was sent straight to a patch of 900 blueberry plants. The farm owner had the only crop of Georgia blueberries in all sub-Saharan Africa, and they required proper care and attention. Matt says he overheard someone say upon his arrival, "Oh, we got the guy to do the blueberries this summer." Perhaps his resume said "Blueberry Intern" for a short period, I'm not sure. Matt's job was twofold: to water the plants religiously and protect them from milli bugs. These little white bugs were destructive to the crops, so he would pick them off and put them in a bucket. This bucket contained a solution of water and dish soap, which would kill them.

In the evenings, he would devote his attention to the local school children. There were not many trees in the area, so he could 'see the kids coming from a mile away.' When they arrived, Matt would tutor them and help them with homework before switching to playing games and teaching them guitar. This group of children was made up of orphans, who didn't always grow up nearby. Many had bounced around, picking up different languages including Afrikaans, Zulu, English, and SiSwati. Describing them, Matt emphasized, "They were geniuses, super able to communicate from a young age. Even if they couldn't speak English well initially, they picked it up after spending a couple weeks with me."

His days were fully packed, and he would start them off early so he could then catch up with Bailey. For the first two weeks of Matt's time there, she was on a mission trip in Oregon, where she couldn't use her phone. She would use a pay phone to call her mom in NC, who would then email him updates. He tried to mail her letters too, but the mail took so long to arrive, he actually beat them back to the US! Turns out, he could have just brought the letters with him on the flight home.

It was a risk to put so much distance between himself and Bailey. Fortunately, all these unique communication challenges strengthened their confidence in the relationship. In future years, they maintained long-distance again, so he could pursue opportunities in DC and San Francisco. When Bailey visited him the summer he was in San Francisco, he proposed. They have been married since the summer of 2020, and I would venture to say a life-altering commitment like that is another bold action.

That summer spent internationally also developed his ability to take care of himself and to find comfort in spending time alone in thought. This emboldened him to take a future job, which involved an hour commute where he was able to spend time thinking to himself. In Nhlangano, he started off completely on his own, but ended up making friends. He made memories like learning how to shoot a slingshot as described in the biblical David and Goliath story. Referencing that moment, Matt attributed, "respect for David, because it is not as easy as I thought it would be."

Matt summed up all this with, "I don't know if that's bold enough, but that's my story." I found that statement both hilarious and painfully humble. This story screams 'bold' to me, yet he still doubted whether it was the type of story I was looking for. I took the opportunity to reinforce several things: 1) yes, this is a bold story, 2) my only requirements for a bold story are the assumption of risk and decision made to take it, and 3) I was so thankful he was willing to share this portion of his life with me. I was shocked I had not heard this story yet, since I knew him during this timeframe. But I was more surprised that he expected me to be looking for something different from our conversation.

I want to encourage you, dear reader… Your boldness may look different than mine, or the stories shared in this book, and that is ok. Risk tolerance varies from person to person, and it is the willingness to take the risk that makes the story interesting.

Matt, like many people, prefers to listen to others' stories, only sharing his own when directly asked. Until recently, I was all too content to share my stories without curiosity for what exciting things my friends could contribute. I am working to be more intentional with my question-asking to learn from the brilliant minds around me and their experiences. What is something you might ask a friend to learn something new about them?

"I'll do it!"

Bailey is an absolute sweetheart. As you have already read, she is married to Matt Q. Our college house referred to her as our "Queen" -her clumsiness might prevent us from calling her naturally graceful, but she is certainly classy, gorgeous, and one of my favorite people. She is artistically and musically gifted, yet never one to draw attention to herself. She is a kind soul and it was no surprise when she announced her new role as a teacher for students with special needs.

Another thing about Bailey has been clear in my years of knowing her: she loves her family and factors them and Matt into her decisions. Knowing this, it is surprising to hear of a major choice she made quickly without consulting them. When Bailey was in her final semester of high school, she started to attend Young Life with a couple of her friends. A couple months later she received a group text from her Young Life leader. Would anyone be able to fill an open position at a Young Life camp? The text included a few key details: 1) the camp was in Oregon, 2) the staff would have to leave the day after graduation to arrive on time, 3) the cost of the flight would not be covered. Bailey read the text and "immediately thought in my head that I wanted to go. Without talking to anybody, not checking dates, without really considering what it would look like for me to be there for a month, I just felt called to do it." Without hesitation or further contemplation, Bailey replied to the group chat, "I'll do it if it's still open!"

This response was completely out of character for Bailey. There were several logistical questions up in the air she would typically want to iron out before making a commitment. She lives by her calendar and traditionally talks to her parents about things like this because she is often afraid she will sign herself up for something she will later want to decline. Despite these tendencies,

Bailey neither second guessed her decision, nor attempted to back out. "I was confident in what I was doing… I don't know what inspired me, but in the moment, I felt called to do it." This was the quickest and most enthusiastic she has ever felt about a decision.

The morning after graduation, Bailey got on a plane by herself for the first time. She was headed to the West Coast for the first time, to a state she had never considered visiting. She was ready to serve in the camp dining hall, setting up and serving groups of students in middle school and high school. But Bailey didn't know anyone else at the camp. On the bus, Bailey felt shy and tired, and she found herself on the outskirts of budding friendships. Bailey felt intimidated, saying, "These people are already best friends and we just arrived at this camp." At camp, everyone turned in their phones, so she could only contact her family and Matt through pay phones. As you read in Matt's story, he was several time zones away in Swaziland. With all of this, she felt lonely the first week at camp.

Fortunately, in the coming weeks, Bailey was able to meet more of the staffers on a personal level through Bible studies and through sharing testimonies. The rest of her time at camp was a time of independence and growth for Bailey. She found her experience meeting people there prepared her for college a couple months later. At school, she felt both more comfortable meeting people and more driven to find a church community. She tested out several different churches and campus ministries on her own, encouraged by her experience at Young Life camp. She stuck with Reformed University Fellowship (RUF), eventually living with several other girls and me. RUF shaped many of her friendships and her faith in the coming years. Bailey reflects, "I don't know if I would have pursued a community like that had I not had the experience in Oregon."

True to the rapidity of Bailey's decision making here, this example of boldness is brief. Often, our bold choices happen instantaneously, without extended periods of contemplation of factors, risk, or reward. For Bailey, that immediate confidence identified the moment as bold compared to her habitual decision-making process. She found it to be a defining and impactful moment, spearheading her future decisions. "Up until that point, I had lived in my comfort zone and that was pushing me outside of my comfort zone."

When have you said "yes!" to something important, without hesitation or strings attached?

"So not me"

Like Bailey, Annalise does not make her decisions in an instant. Annalise is extremely thoughtful with her words, actions, and plans. She is practical and a perfectionist by nature, which has always been a fun element in our friendship. While I don't exactly fly by the seat of my pants, I do find it comical to see her reactions to my more outrageous stories and ideas.

Annalise's boldness over the last several years has compounded, shaping her decision process today. When Annalise was wrapping up her time at a small K-12 Christian school, she was used to a small class with only 13 other girls. She received college acceptances from her parents' alma maters, another school where her best friends were going, and one that would be completely new. As she contemplated her options, she knew she would be more comfortable at something smaller, or at a Christian college. But, she decided the transition post-grad wouldn't be as drastic if she chose to attend a school that wasn't made up of people who already agreed on faith. Choosing a larger, more diverse institution would give her a chance to challenge herself, asking questions like: "is this really what I believe?"

Annalise decided to go to UNC, embracing the assumption it would push her. She was right; it did push her. Annalise's first year was challenging, especially socially. Stepping out of her comfort zone left her feeling defeated and emotional. She reflects, "I did this totally new thing, and I was so homesick, I cried every day. I didn't know how to do college. I was so frustrated I considered going back home to do community college." After some 'tough love' from her dad, she decided to stick it out. She journaled and sought out Christian community, settling in at RUF. She started to spend time with other first-year students, being intentional about making plans. Even when she started to have a regular friend group, Annalise began to have social anxiety. She was plagued with internal questions like, "do they like me? Do I deserve to be here?" One day, she confessed to a girl she had met, "I do things with people, but I don't know if we're friends." To this, the girl across the table said, "we're friends, right?" This girl's reassurance helped Annalise get out of her head and enjoy her blossoming friendships.

Fast forward a few semesters, well after Annalise established her own routine and had established a group of "her people," she found herself facing another opportunity to make a bold choice. Annalise and I were sitting at a picnic table, mapping out our classes for the remaining semesters. I was in the position to finish my required coursework a semester prior to graduation but planned to stay on campus as a part-time student, taking a couple extra classes instead of graduating early. I was in love with the school and was intent on spending all eight semesters there, saying, "why would I want to leave?" My plan surprised Annalise, but the conversation and our mapping of classes helped her realize she, too, could have a semester open. Her idea to use that semester, however, was to study abroad. There was only one place that Annalise wanted to go: the Netherlands. She had family there and wanted to connect with her family history.

Annalise chose a program through the business school. She couldn't ask any of her friends in different majors to do the program with her, so she would be travelling with a group of students she didn't know. Learning from her experience of moving to UNC without a built-in community, she felt confident. She trusted God would provide community, like He had done for her before. Annalise took the knowledge her previous experience had taught her, to feel comfortable making another leap. She left the continent for the first time during her junior, spring semester.

When she arrived, Annalise turned to her habit of journaling to process her situation, like she had in her first year at UNC. She started to be more spontaneous, often making weekend trips alone to different cities or to meet up with distant relatives. She describes being alone as, "so not me." My extroverted self feels that on a deep level. In school, Annalise would spend most of her day with friends, even getting ready in the mornings with her roommate. In Amsterdam, she would take several bold steps to do things on her own, like taking the train by herself. She would go to places alone in her regular routine, like the grocery store. She laughs thinking about the time she needed nail polish remover and relied heavily on Google Translate to find it in the aisles with Dutch descriptions. Another time, she biked to a Christian student ministry, making friends outside her program.

That summer, Annalise moved to Charlotte for a summer internship. She didn't know her coworkers or roommates, but trusted like both college and study abroad, everything would work out, and it did.

Fast forward to the summer after graduation, when Annalise moved to Greenville, SC. Not only was she in a new city, but also in a job that was very different than what she ever imagined herself in. This "crazy job" involved driving a company pickup truck to Home Depots and selling power tools. Even with this job, Annalise's transition to Greenville was one of her easiest yet when it comes to building community, and she knows she wants to stay for the time being. Looking back, she knows there is no way she would have had such an easy transition to Greenville "if it wasn't for the last four years." Her bold choices have helped her learn how to approach situations on her own, how to "be an adult and make new friends." Each choice had "just enough change and difficulty with a little bit of comfort," helping shape her into a more courageous version of herself.

What previous experiences in your life have made you more optimistic when facing challenges today?

Natural State of Shyness

Like Annalise, Sara went through an experience where she forced herself into a new community. Sara is famous among our friends for several things: being obsessed with golden retrievers, having an abnormally large head that is prone to concussions, and laughing at fart jokes. In 2022, Sara will graduate from law school and get married, moving forward significantly in life stages despite her self-proclaimed immaturity. In addition to sharing many laughs, Sara and I have shared both joy and sorrow in our personal lives and in the outcome of sporting events.

In high school, Sara had a specific plan. She always wanted to attend UNC and was "so fast-paced and single-track minded, I didn't let anything intrude on that space." Sara didn't bother touring any colleges, her mind was made up. She did, however, apply to a few other prestigious schools to see if she would be accepted. Some acceptance letters started to roll in, including one from UNC. Then came a letter making her hesitate for a moment. She opened the email from NYU while she was in New York City for spring break. At that moment, Sara was on the tail end of a magical week. She loved NYC, but did she want to live there? Her contemplation was fleeting; the tuition difference was so drastic that Sara didn't think much more of it.

In her first year at UNC, Sara experienced lots of happy moments without needing to leave her comfort zone. She didn't need to challenge her natural state of shyness because she had a large base of familiar faces from our high school. Often, Sara would know at least one person when she showed up on the first day of a class or activity. Plus, her parents were a short 30- minute drive away and if anything would ever go wrong, she could call them for help.

In February of her first year, Sara discovered a flyer advertising 6-week summer classes at NYU. She remembers thinking to herself, "this is a really good compromise." The tuition for one French class would be much more manageable than that of full-time, so she could test out the school she had been so curious about previously. "I'll get my fix, then I'll be ready to go home."

If she went to NYU, she would be leaving her comfort zone behind. 19-year-old Sara didn't know anyone who lived in the NYC area and would have to "put myself out there to make friends." She would be in flying-distance away from her parents. She wouldn't be able to investigate her apartment before moving in. She had heard "horror stories of New York being dangerous" and she hadn't ever explored the NYU campus or its surrounding area. All in all, she knew it would be "very different than the one year I've lived away from home."

In an act of boldness, Sara enrolled in her NYU class for the summer and found a studio apartment. She was both excited and terrified as she travelled north to move in. She turned the keys, unlocking the door to her room that was much smaller and dirtier than she had imagined. The fear hit her all at once and it "took everything in my power to not sob in front of my dad." When he left, she broke down. Her first four hours were spent crying and bleaching her apartment. Exhausted, she thought to herself, "this is stupid. I'm not going to sit here and cry for six weeks." She took a break and left the apartment for a walk. She explored her nearby area and found a "fat donut" which helped her mood dramatically. She was able to rediscover her original infatuation with the hustle and bustle of the city.

After her "4-hour sob fest" and re-centering walk, Sara "hit the ground running." But it was hardly all smooth sailing. She started to get the hang of public transportation, but occasionally found herself on the wrong train. Her class started and she "didn't know a single soul." Until now, Sara had "never really put myself out there enough to go up to a random person and make friends." She sometimes felt like she had been "thrown into the deep end."

She found it scary to interact with the strangers in her program, but reasoned, "if I don't push myself outside of my comfort zone, it's going to be a pretty lonely summer." Sara was relieved to find "people were a lot more receptive than I expected." As she talked to the other students, she learned many of them were looking for friends, too. Many of them were from different backgrounds; they were just as curious about her experience at UNC as she was about their experiences.

That summer, Sara explored much more of what the city had to offer. Much of her adventuring was through solo walks, a habit that still persists today. She had a blast that summer, loving NYC even more than before. She even considered transferring to NYU. This time in thought made her more introspective and brought her to the conclusion of staying at UNC.

Sara's experience moving to NYC and making friends without a built-in support system was bold for her at the time. But since she has faced those specific risks, she would not find it as bold of a choice if repeated today. Her comfort zone has expanded over the years as a result of her bold choices.

How has your comfort zone expanded?

Quitter and Proud of It

The previous travel stories include risk, in part because travel, especially solo travel, was novel for that person. For James, who grew up traveling, boldness doesn't come in on the travel aspect itself. It was more about what he was choosing to leave.

To a stranger, James might not stand out from the crowd as he is a white male with brown hair. But it brings tears to my eyes when I think about how sweet it is to have friends as great as James. He is loyal to a fault, especially when it comes to his boys, his family, and his sports teams. He's scrappy and diligent, throwing himself headfirst into his work. He's generous with his money, time, and words. Perhaps most of all, James is an utter goofball. My mind floods with memories shared with this dear friend: watching sports, taking road trips, partying, eating at his favorite hole-in-the wall restaurants like Cosmic Cantina, or doing absolutely nothing at all.

When I thought about who embodied boldness, I thought of James. He is a confident man with exciting stories from across the globe. Shoot, he has even run with the bulls! Surprisingly, James showed extreme resistance referring to any of his decisions as bold. He humbly says, "bold suggests some consciously risky decision, and I don't want to give myself that much credit when I was really just feeling the moment." He recognizes many privileges in his life that afforded him confidence everything would work out for him, and he would have some sort of safety net or support system to pick him back up if he ever fell. Because of that, none of his decisions felt bold in the moment. I continue to encourage him we all have different factors in our lives which embolden us, but recognizing those factors does not rule out the possibility for boldness.

After many discussions, James thought of a decision that could be bold in a 'not-so-stereotypically positive understanding' of the word.

During his junior year of college, James saw an opportunity to apply for assistant sports editor for the Daily Tar Heel (DTH), our campus newspaper. He was already a senior writer and would be a reasonable choice for the role, but he knew the time commitment would be more than what he wanted, so he didn't apply. Later, the DTH editors directly asked him to apply, but he said no. He chose to keep his focus on his course load, his friends, his girlfriend, and his officer position on the club cross country team. He was happy with his choice. But when the DTH editors invited him to dinner, they started speaking as if he had accepted the position. He was confused, he had not applied, so how had he accidentally agreed to take it? It turns out he did not, but they needed someone to take on the role, so they simply told James it was him!

On top of his other commitments, James was now spending 30-40 hours a week working for the DTH, often traveling to cover events. Very quickly, it became stressful. To compensate for his new scarcity of time, he stopped sleeping. He continued to show up for his club team and for his friends, but he was slowly becoming less and less of the energetic and smiley James we all knew. Two months in, it was too much. James started to consider dropping out of school, backing out of everything all at once, and embarking upon a solitary semester abroad. He had several positive traveling experiences and believed time abroad was what he needed to break free and reset. He said "my tank was empty. Making it to December was going to take everything I had within me."

At the last second, he had the opportunity to join a program in London. He had known about it, but initially held off because his girlfriend was attending, and he didn't want to step on her toes. When he asked her about it, they agreed it would be good for him to join instead of venturing on his solo trip.

Come spring semester, James quit all his commitments on campus. He quit the DTH and his position with club cross country, got on a plane and left the country. While quitting may not be the first example you think of for the word "bold," James confidently chose to do what was best for himself and his health, risking losing face or respect from those he cared about. In his words, "No one wants to bail on a commitment, it makes you look like a coward. I felt committed to everything: club cross country, DTH, friends, housemates. But I knew it was too much… I had to have the balls to say I couldn't do this." While he was fortunate to go through his challenging semester without added pressures of anxiety or depression, he still "felt like there was no escape." So, he ran away to do just that: escape.

When he got to London, it didn't end up being the freeing experience he had idealized in his mind. He was consistently frustrated with the job he found there. His girlfriend was going through the hardest time in her life, often staying up until 3 or 4 in the morning crying. James would stay up with her, hoping to be a source of comfort. Understandably, it all took a toll on him. James realized his bold choice to quit his commitments and go to London might not have paid off as he had hoped.

Seeking a second chance at the whole escape and self-discovery thing, James found a summer internship in Barcelona. He didn't know anyone else who would be in Barcelona, but he was ready to make friends with his coworkers. When he arrived in Barcelona, he emailed his boss, asking when and where he should plan to start on his first day. He never got a response, so he showed up at the office on Monday morning. No one was there. Confused, James called his boss. Turns out, he was not going to work from any office at all. He would work remotely from his apartment, which was unusual before the COVID-19 pandemic. Unsure of how he could meet people, he would often go weeks on end without spending time with other people or speaking in English – and he was not fluent in Spanish. He spent the majority of the next two months on his own; reading, walking, and talking to friends and family on the phone.

His eight months in Europe, split between London and Barcelona, did not turn out to be the escape he was looking for. He backed out on his commitments and didn't love the place he found himself in afterwards. This is the thing about taking risks: they don't always pay off, and no matter how badly I want to, I can't claim every bold decision works out. The risk is what makes the decision bold in the first place. Thankfully, many people find their failures and risks realized, as well as challenges in life, set them up for their most valuable lessons.

In that regard, James says those eight months were the best thing that could have happened to him. "What would I have learned if it worked out how I wanted it to?" During this time, James learned what he needed to. He missed his support structure, and often felt even lonelier when his social interaction had to be planned out in advance because of time zone differences, like slotting his name into someone else's calendar. He missed "mindlessly wasting time with those he loves." He longed for simple interactions in person, like grabbing a beer with a buddy, going on a run with a friend, or grabbing dinner with his mom.

Maybe after the COVID-19 pandemic, many more of you can resonate with such longings.

After his many months abroad, we welcomed our good pal James back to North Carolina. We couldn't get enough of him during senior year. He was often found at his house, the North Star, "mindlessly wasting time" with his housemates. In his final semester, James ran into a friend who asked him to live with him in Boston next year. James didn't have a job lined up yet, but that was not his concern. He now knew the main thing he needed was an in-person network of people, and he could figure out the rest. His sister lived there already, and a few other friends were also moving to Boston, so after a day or so, James signed the lease. I would also call that decision bold, but for him, it didn't feel like much of a risk at all, because he had some guaranteed community there. As it happened, James was offered a job and had to move to Boston earlier than his lease started, in order to make his first day at work.

I know this isn't the end of the conversation with James. He's not satisfied with the examples of boldness in his life, even the one outlined here. He wants to do more to live up to the word. He wants to be bolder going forward. While I'm frustrated, he doesn't recognize the boldness already there, the past boldness is not the end goal. I fight hard to point out past examples of boldness so my friends and family will believe they can do it again. To make it more real, instead of a lofty, unspecific goal to be bold and take risks. So, James, I hope you can use these moments that don't feel quite bold enough to you, and have a better idea of what would. You, my friend, are and can be bold.

My favorite line from this conversation with James is, "I was a quitter and I'm proud of it." When have you said no to something, setting firm boundaries to focus on your priorities? When have you taken a risk for the only payoff to be a lesson learned?

<u>3</u>

Time of Transition

Throughout several of the bold stories I've heard, there is a pattern: they happened at periods of transition in the person's life. When people were brainstorming what their potential bold stories would be, I often encouraged them to think of transitions they had experienced, to see if there was anything particularly challenging or risky about that transition. There can be much discomfort in transitions when you are navigating a new circumstance. How you choose to handle that discomfort can be an effort to build walls up and protect yourself, keeping things as they were as much as possible. Or, you can choose to embrace the change and make the best of it, even if it is difficult. Several of the upcoming stories show examples of boldness in embracing a change and diving into a transition.

In other upcoming stories, it turns out their transitions were a result of a bold choice. Sometimes, one decision can change the trajectory of your life, whether you knew about the significance in that moment or not. Choosing something, whether it be a habit, goal, or perspective, then sticking to it, can change what our life looks like and what possibilities there will be going forward.

8 Years of Solitude

If you know me well, you know I think my grandparents are the cutest people ever. I love talking about them, frequently whipping out my favorite picture, where my grandpa is proudly wearing a bowtie that my grandma made for him. Denton is not related to me by blood, but he is the truest grandfather figure I could ever hope for. Right after graduation, I moved to Chicago, and he looked up the Chicago weather every single morning thinking of me. What a sweetheart! When I think of him, I conjure up memories of him performing with his flute group, being more excited about the topic of calculus than I could ever be, and many meals where he wore a yellow shirt and spilled some sort of red sauce on it. I like to think I take after him in all three of those situations, playing flute for four years, learning for fun, and believing the best meals are also the messiest.

My grandpa is rather reserved, and in recent years, I have been intentionally asking him questions about his life. He continues to blow me away. While I knew he had lived on a boat for a period, and remember spending one night on the boat myself, I was shocked to learn he lived on a boat for 15 years in total. While I knew my grandma was not his first wife, I was surprised to learn she wasn't his second either. She was his fourth. Wow, he's lived such an eventful life, and for most of mine, I had not thought to ask him about it.

I interviewed him when we celebrated his 90th birthday, and his first statement was, "I don't do anything bold and that's intentional. That's how I have lived to be 90." When I clarified that not all bold actions are life threatening, and many of the stories I heard have been emotional, he decided he did indeed have a story to share with me.

After his previous wife died from a health condition, my grandpa was left alone to grieve a monumental loss. As one can imagine, he had a hard time coping, turning to a variety of things that failed to fill the new void in his heart. One day, when he and his boss took their normal lunch break to watch the boats in the harbor, his boss suggested Denton buy a boat. A boat could give him something in his life to devote his attention and thoughts toward, allowing his focus to eventually change to something else. He decided to go for it. He bought a boat, and once he hit retirement, he moved onto it. Believe it or not, that is not the boldness he would like to highlight.

He lived on his boat for the next eight years in solitude. He would go back and forth between Morehead City, NC, and the Florida Keys, depending on the weather. He would make polite small talk with the attendants when he stopped for fuel or a meal, and even picked up the occasional drinking buddy at the docks. But mostly, he was alone, and preferred to keep it that way. He had closed himself off from others, fearing any relationship or friendship could lead to a repetition of the enormous loss he already knew too well.

One evening, when he was docked in Morehead City, one of his acquaintances rode up on her bike to invite him to a dinner party she was hosting. Initially, he saw it as a 'dangerous thing,' interacting with others. In fact, the night of the event, he called to back out. But the host was not the one to answer the phone; her friend picked it up instead. This friend of hers, Karen, insisted he join them. With this forceful encouragement, he decided to attend. That, ladies and gentlemen, was Denton's bold moment, even if a slightly reluctant one! He chose to open himself back up to human connection when he had intentionally avoided it for so long. He describes the danger of human connection as partly, "I lived such a solitary existence, it made me nervous to be around people. I didn't want to have conversations." Inserting yourself into a room full of new people and making small talk can bring awkwardness and social anxiety for many. I imagine this hesitation and discomfort must have been amplified tenfold for my grandpa because of his solitary lifestyle. Yet he chose to attend, he decided he was ready to open himself back up.

So, Denton boldly biked over to his first dinner party in years. The group sat around a table and shared a meal. Afterwards, he got up and helped wash the dishes, which impressed Karen, the woman he spoke to on the phone. When he finished, she invited him to talk with her on the porch - they ended up talking for hours. Eventually, she put his bike in her car and drove him back to his boat. "I liked her and the way she thought; I wanted to see her again," so he set a date with her for the upcoming weekend. You can guess where this is going next, right? They became more significant in each other's lives and he proposed. Karen was a single mom, and by the time she and Denton got married, her daughter Christine was in college. If you remember, Christine is my mom. Everything comes back to ME, doesn't it?

In all seriousness, my grandparents have been married for over 25 years. My grandpa says, "sometimes things happen to you in life without you seeking or planning it out. I've decided the Lord gets involved... I think it was an outside force that brought us together."

When have you found yourself faced with an opportunity you weren't necessarily looking for? When have you said yes, even though you felt a little nervous about it?

Living Aboard

It only makes sense for the next introduction to be my grandma, Karen. She's an energetic entrepreneur, and I would be remiss if I didn't shout out her Etsy shop: The Quilting Mandarin. If you like bright colors, she's your gal. I would certainly call her fashion choices bold, but maybe it is just the age difference talking. In recent years, I have moved further from my grandparents geographically, but I hear from them often enough and surprisingly feel as close as ever. My grandma is an author of eight books, and now she channels her passion for words into a daily email to a list of five recipients including my mom and myself.

The details of her bold story can be found in her book, Carolina Comfort II. If you were paying attention in the last story, you will remember my grandpa was living on a boat when my grandma met him. After they got married, he began convincing her to go on 'months of freedom' where they would sojourn up and down the East Coast on his boat.

Like most of us, she had a life on land. This included a job, church involvements, regular nail salon appointments, a house with a yard, and possessions like furniture and family heirlooms. While their frequent monthly cruises taught her more and more about sailing, it still took her a while to feel at ease on the boat. For five years, she settled into a routine of regular sailing excursions. She was growing increasingly prepared to make the bold jump of living on the boat full-time. When she retired, they decided to go for it. The change was so drastic it took six months to make all the preparations.

Without any income, they sold their second car. The boat had significantly less storage space than she had in her house, so she had to sell or give away most of her things, including all of her 'power suits' for work. In fact, she only brought three pairs of shoes with her on the boat. Grandma describes her downsizing as more than just all the clothes, "We got rid of things, responsibilities, ties to the community and acquaintances. Neighborhood squabbles, international politics, violent books, and gory movies were eliminated from our sphere." Their lifestyle would change, in activities and in social interaction. Most significant was the decision to move away from family. This was one of the biggest factors keeping her from moving on full-time; she reasons, "My aging parents lived next door and I was a grandmother. I couldn't live on a boat."

Despite all the changes required, she did move onto the boat with Grandpa. They stayed there for five years, and as I mentioned before, they had occasional guests. Even as a small child, I remember tight sleeping quarters; I can attest they were hardly staying on a yacht! What the boat lacked in space, it made up for with a "waterfront view." They "discovered small coastal towns, made life-long friends, and shared extreme moments of fear. We have endured El Nino winters on the west coast of Florida, Lake Okeechobee droughts and endless nights of bouncing, hull-slapping, anchorages. We have stayed at delightful quirky marinas." They have made memories to tide them over in the coming years... pun intended! Her biggest takeaway of all was that she and Grandpa "formed a 'more perfect union' blending into one distinct spirit while cruising."

Describing their later decision to settle in New Bern, NC, she explained, "When the boat seemed like more work than fun, we decided to sell." After all the time "living aboard," she summarizes, "I miss the journey, but not the boat." Since moving back onto land in 2002, their journeys are more likely to be road trips, visiting our family or attending a flute festival or quilting convention. Even now, they are minimalists, selling or giving away things they don't use often. They don't even keep a Christmas tree anymore, hanging up a quilt of a Christmas tree that Grandma made so it doesn't take up as much space.

Moving onto a boat full-time and selling most of her worldly possessions was a radically bold decision. Yes, she had several things going for her, making herself more confident in that choice, including a husband who had previously done so for years, and having some experience on the water herself. With that confidence, she committed fully, changing the course of her life. I hope, when I retire, to follow in their footsteps and live on a boat for at least a month and see how it goes from there. I would bet if I asked, they would both still be able to teach me how to tie the different knots. I will save that for the next visit.

How have you taken a passion and dove into it head-first? When have you "put all your eggs in one basket"?

Type 3 Fun

Another person who has lived in uncommon spots is my dear friend and outdoors inspiration, Jake. He was one of the first people I got to know in college, and he has always been down for what he calls, "type 2 fun." Type 2 fun involves much more effort and grit than normal or, "type 1 fun." One of our type 2 fun adventures was my first backpacking trip, where I returned covered in blisters. Jake has done tons of adventuring on his own, documenting everything in detail through self-timer photos and goofy commentary. His experiences encourage me to plan more adventures for myself. If Jake can put in the effort to explore, so can I! Well, I am not so sure I can use that logic anymore, because in the summer of 2021, Jake hiked the Pacific Crest Trail (PCT). That means he hiked 2,650 miles continuously, stretching the length from Mexico to Canada. He's officially found himself on the "type 3 fun" bandwagon.

To many, quitting his job as a software engineer and spending five months on the PCT appears bold. But Jake said it was "not that bold for me". The PCT had "always intrigued me," and Jake knew he would do it over two years prior to his start date. Jake had been thorough with his plans. He had never loved the company he worked for, and counted down the days until he could move on to the next thing. "When I started the PCT, I wasn't even very nervous. It was all just part of the plan."

When Jake told family and friends about his plan to hike the PCT, they were unanimously supportive. But when one of their follow-up questions included, "What are you thinking of doing with your life afterwards?" Jake didn't have a plan and would jokingly retreat, saying, "don't ask me that right now." Fortunately for him, he could contemplate his answer over the next five months while alone on the trail.

In his first couple hundred miles, Jake knew he didn't want to dive back into a full-time corporate setting. He didn't want to rush back into a norm he never enjoyed in the first place. He didn't want his months on the trail to fade into memories of adventure, its significance reducing as his years behind a desk accumulated. He didn't want to go back to that norm and eventually behave as though he never left. Jake could already see the trail had changed him.

Jake's priorities had always been based on his experiences outside the office, or outside any building, if possible. He would minimize his time in front of TV's, except for UNC sporting events, and explore the nature surrounding his city. But as he continued to hike north, he knew he wanted to utilize the remainder of his savings to delay his return to a full-time job. He wanted to act on his priorities, intentionally using his time to "keep traveling, keep pursuing new experiences." Initially, Jake was excited by the idea of southeastern Asia, a place he had never been. But as he stopped in towns along the trail and heard news updates of the delta variant of COVID-19 rampant worldwide, he realized international travel would not be feasible for the time being.

Jake reached the California / Oregon border and felt lost, but not physically. He didn't know how or where he would continue to seek out adventures and exciting experiences. Did he need to get a job to make ends meet while he figured it out?

With surprising speed for a man traveling by foot, Jake arrived in Bend, Oregon. He had been there twice before, first with his family when he was immediately enamored with the place. He had wanted to live there, but had not found any job opportunities relevant to his career after he graduated. He was bummed, but found a way to visit Bend a second time, during a solo cross-country road trip. He had stayed at a hostel with "incredible vibes" and left again, convinced it was the "coolest place ever." Returning to this town he loved, he stayed a few nights in the hostel he found previously.

As Jake was sitting in the hostel courtyard, observing an open mic night, he couldn't help but ask himself, "Why am I not coming here for the winter and working here?" But "something was holding me back. I didn't want to commit to that." Jake was afraid of putting his career on pause for additional months and wrestled with the idea internally.

During his stay, Jake made a stop at REI. He started chatting with the cashier; she happened to also be from North Carolina. They "seemed to really connect there for a couple minutes," and when he eventually walked away, he regretted not asking for her phone number. She had a pretty unique name, so he was able to find her on Instagram and messaged her. Jake thought it was "a little bold on my part," and was confused after 24 hours went by without a response.

But then she responded! They made plans to grab a drink that night, and Jake was ecstatic. In a rollercoaster of emotions, she cancelled on him a few hours later. He was bummed, because he had to continue his journey north and couldn't wait for them to reschedule. Since Jake spent most of his days alone with his thoughts on the trail, his interactions in the towns along the way "get amplified...they become your life... I was way more invested in this whole interaction than I probably should have been."

That's when he decided to come back to Bend for the winter. "Why not?" It had given him another opportunity to connect with this girl. For the first time in his life, Jake was "structuring a life decision around a girl," which felt bold. Realistically, there was a chance nothing would work out between him and the cashier, so Jake questioned what else was there in Bend to make the move worth it. But he knew, "everything is here for me." Bend was a place where Jake could "make being an outdoorsman a priority." He could "find a community of people like me that are kind of nomadic and put their life experiences over their careers." He could live and work at the hostel he loved, and could ski throughout the winter. So, Jake decided to commit to this plan and when he shared the story with me, he was on the road driving out there.

Jake found boldness in "deciding the direction I want my life to move toward... If I don't do it now, when will I ever do it?" From now on, Jake plans to make an effort to pursue adventures, regardless of the excuses. "It's not a totally new part of me, but I'm following through."

Jake has now discovered the girl from REI is now dating someone else. So much for his first life decision based on a girl. Huge bummer. Despite that, Jake had a plethora of reasons to be excited about Bend. If nothing else, she had catalyzed his decision to move there.

While his parents are supportive, Jake's choice to work at the hostel and ski in his free time is "venturing into the territory of less socially accepted." While he was hiking on the PCT, he learned to be alright with not fitting in. With infrequent showers, he smelled and appeared like a "homeless person, basically." He states, "If I'm going to be a ski bum and you don't like it, well, too bad. That is what I want to do."

Jake felt bold because at the end of his hiking trip, he had countless doors he could open. "I could do anything," so choosing to commit to Bend felt significant. "I will eventually go back and get a software engineering job," but he is not going to wait for someone to give him their approval to do what he wants in the meantime. "I don't feel entirely comfortable with that all the time, but I'm getting there...the edge of my comfort zone." Jake is becoming more confident in his actions because they align with his priorities, even if they are out of order for someone else. He is hoping the people he meets in Bend will have similar priorities and lifestyles to his.

When have you done something a little unconventional? When have you confidently committed to one path of several?

Jazzed About Religion

Next, I would like to introduce you to my friend Manthi. Like the last few stories, her boldness created a major transition in her life. Her identity has changed, not just her circumstances. Manthi and I lived in the same suite freshman year of college, and she had a bubbly, loud energy. I loved spending time with her, but once we moved the following year, our busy schedules got the better of us. We reconnected when I moved to Charlotte for work.

While we might have started off discussing safe topics like Manthi's recent acceptance into medical school and my rotations in Chicago and SoCal, it didn't end there. When we talked about the difficulties of friendships and working during the pandemic, Manthi was incredibly authentic. She was honest about discovering how her patients' deaths impacted her emotionally. She was vulnerable about what she went through when her mentor, Mr. Steve, died the week before her medical school interview. She shared with me that during college, she had become a Christian, and how that transformed her entire life.

The next week we reconvened, and Manthi shared her bold story, which happens to be her transition from Buddhism to Christianity. As I mentioned earlier, I don't expect all my readers to agree on the topic of faith, but I also can't ignore or attempt to diminish something that is such a large piece in Manthi's individual testimony.

Manthi is Sri Lankan and grew up going to a Buddhist temple with her family. But from the time she was about eight years old, she started to contemplate the possibility of a God. She had never heard anyone talk about God, but she had this question in the back of her mind. She continued to attend Buddhist temples for most of her life, "going through the motions." For Manthi, this meant she was attending and participating in the ways expected of her. Outwardly, a stranger might not recognize anything out of the ordinary with her faith. But inwardly, she didn't feel the sense of passion or belief she had heard others describe. She was aware something just didn't click.

Over many years while she went through the motions, her thoughts about the possibility of God increased. Looking back, she states, "God pursued me while I pursued him. He infiltrated my thoughts and conversations in a way I could not ignore." She started to pray and ask for signs. I imagine some readers may not believe in signs, but I encourage you to keep reading, nevertheless. This is part of Manthi's unique story, providing an example of her boldness and some reassurance that gave her confidence to continue to be bold.

One day, after Manthi spent hours studying for a test, frequently searching for answers to her questions on Google, she became frustrated. Pre-med courses are no joke, and at this point in her studies, Manthi was starting to question if it was all worth it. She questioned whether she should keep her major, if it made any sense for her to put in the effort to become a pediatrician. She prayed, and might I add, more boldly than I have. She asked for a sign - not of God's existence, but if she was on the right career path. She asked if she might be shown something - anything, that could indicate whether she was meant to be a doctor. Then she went back to studying. She returned to the homepage of Google, and lo and behold, the artwork was of a woman treating a child and wearing a stethoscope. Manthi had been on that page so many times that day and didn't notice the image until right after her prayer. For Manthi, this image of Fe Del Mundo, the first woman to be admitted to Harvard Medical School, represented instantaneous reassurance she was on the right path. Someone else might interpret this as a coincidence, but as for Manthi and me, we don't believe in coincidences. The sign created renewed confidence in Manthi's decision to pursue a relationship with God.

Halfway through our senior year of college, Manthi boldly decided to have a conversation with her mom, letting her in on everything she had been considering regarding faith. She trusted her mom would be receptive, but it was still a conversation she was nervous about. This was the biggest thing going on in Manthi's life, and she wanted to share it with her mom in a way that would not diminish the religion in which her mom had raised her. When they talked, Manthi described it to her mom as, "the way you feel about temple is the way I feel about God. I want a relationship; I want to learn more about Him." As they were talking, her mom was supportive and wanted to understand; no one had talked to her about God before either. Manthi describes it as a "beautiful conversation, but it was a scary moment. I had never talked to her about something like that before; I didn't know how she would react. She was so intentional about asking me questions. She saw the changes in me but had never seen me this jazzed about something like religion."

Spurred on by the positive conversation with her mom, Manthi decided to go to church. She went to an international church and even though she was walking side by side with a friend, she felt afraid. As a newcomer, she felt like she didn't know what to expect. She didn't have the right words to say. Facing those fears of being the "odd man out," she showed up. The church's internal perimeter was lined with flags from across the globe, and the first one in the building was the Sri Lankan flag. Seeing the familiar flag quickly gave her comfort; she "felt like God was taking care of this fear of mine, and I was able to appreciate the unique diversity of that church." Believing she was safe in that moment encouraged her to keep pursuing this new journey. A few months later, Manthi decided to accept Jesus Christ as her savior.

There are several parts in Manthi's story where she felt afraid, or where she didn't know if or how to continue. With a little help, she was able to keep going, opening herself up to something which had previously been so unknown to her. Sometimes that help came in the form of family, friends, strangers, physical signs, or hard-to-explain moments of reassurance and peace. The presence of help doesn't negate the boldness of Manthi's choices. No one was forcing her to do anything - she could have ignored any one of these instruments of assistance, or simply not even recognized them. She could have decided, even with encouragement, the risk and the change were too great. Yet, she accepted the support offered to her and dove into a faith that defines her day-to-day.

When have you made a bold decision or accepted a challenge, reassured by someone else or something around you?

Scared of Ferris Wheels

Sometimes, how we respond to a major transition can be a measure of boldness. We can either tackle the challenges of change head-on, or we can coast by, minimizing our risk. Jackie embraced a couple challenges during his transition to college, with surprising results.

Jackie is one of my closest companions. We love all the same things, so for years we have attended classes, events, and activities together. One of the more unique things we got into was swing dancing. We attempted a flip move and he dropped me on my head. TWICE. Unsurprisingly, we have not tried that move since! I guess you could say that was one bold attempt that didn't work out well.

In his younger years, Jackie was shy. He was aware early on he was different from others. He's Asian; his parents immigrated to the US when they were in their twenties. "Making friends was always hit or miss" and going into college, Jackie "didn't really know anybody." This put him in a new and challenging position. Fortunately, he was invited to an event with a group of guys at the Eno River.

"I didn't realize what it was until I got there." The group planned to cliff jump into the quarry, and "if you know me, I get scared of Ferris wheels, so jumping purposefully into deep water from a high area is not something I normally do for fun. My worst fears include falling and being really high up," which is exactly the scenario he found himself in. Oh boy.

There were a few guys standing off to the side, opting not to jump. With the small group forming, he knew he wouldn't be made fun of if he decided not to jump either. Yet, as each jumper safely landed in the water, Jackie grew increasingly confident. He reasoned, "There's not any particular reason I should fail at this," when compared to those who had gone before him. Boldly, he jumped into the water. He had confronted his fear of falling. But, in his fixation on the act of jumping, he "didn't even think about the fact that he was a bad swimmer." He found himself facing an altogether different fear. When he later discovered a pair of floaties, he quickly donned them for extra buoyancy.

These physical fears were combined with social fears of going into a new situation with all new people. He assumed the only reason he was invited was because some of them knew his sister. He worried if the guys thought he was uncool it would ruin her reputation. He assumed all of them were friends with each other, making him nervous about joining in and inconveniencing them.

Later that week, Jackie found himself in another scenario where he was afraid of inconveniencing people with his friendship. He attended a school event alone, content to keep to himself, but still wanting to check out the festivities. During the event, he saw a girl he thought he recognized. He contemplated whether he should go talk to her. Was it too weird? He typically felt uncomfortable going up and talking to people, especially if it looked like they already had friends. This girl was with her roommate, so he had to work up the nerve to walk over, potentially interrupting their conversation. He boldly went up and started talking to her. But she wasn't the person he thought she was. It was a completely different girl. Whoops, awkward. "Obviously, it turned out really badly."

I laugh when I visualize this story in my head because this is very 'on brand' for Jackie today. He frequently assumes he has recognized someone only to realize they are not the person he thought they were.

But the story doesn't end there. Jackie kept talking to this girl and her roommate, with the intention of making friends. They discovered they all lived in the same building, and the girls gave him an open invitation to visit their suite. Jackie found taking that next step to visit the suite, "which is basically their house" took both confidence and boldness. So, he did it.

He started to be a frequent presence in the suite, growing close to the roommate pair. It so happens the duo were my suitemates, and this bold story conveniently doubles as how Jackie and I met. While his initial interaction was based on a mistake, his boldness resulted in the development of several good friends and the status of "honorary suitemate." He felt "God really worked through that," and throughout college, he saw growth in his confidence and efforts to make plans with people. He is now less nervous making new friends because he started to see his presence was not an inconvenience or bothersome. He has seen instead, "people want me there even if I just met them... I am more confident in what I have to offer other people as a friend."

These two events at the beginning of his first year of college impacted his interactions with strangers today, and gave him friendships he continues to maintain, but he is still very much afraid of heights! He vows he will never skydive, but that is ok. Being bold does not always mean something as drastic as jumping from an airplane. Sometimes, saying "hi" will do the trick.

When have you pushed past fear or awkwardness in a social situation?

4

Releasing Control

While I initially sought out actions as the crux of a bold moment, it is more accurate to call it a choice. Sometimes, the bold choice is to refrain from action. Sometimes, the boldest thing you can do is to stay put, embracing the current discomfort. To accept your current path and stay true to course, even if it is scary. To relinquish control, even if you never truly had it to begin with. To ask for help and then trust whoever is in control isn't making a mistake and you don't need to take over with your own agenda.

Self-imposed Restrictions

My roommate is also named Rachel, so our friends in Charlotte now refer to us as 'the Rachels'. Sometimes, to avoid confusion, we just go by RG and RH. Some words frequently used in RH's vocabulary are "delight," "sweet friend," and "hoot and a half." Funnily enough, I could use all three of those phrases to describe her. Rachel and I have rapidly become close friends, and she has been incredibly supportive of my bold interviews. Now it is her turn to share her story.

During one of her summer breaks while she was a student at Georgia Tech, Rachel went to an Avett Brothers concert in Denver. Halfway through the concert, she was suddenly nauseous and couldn't breathe. She had to leave the concert early, and even when she was flying back home the next day she felt 'outside of herself.' Rachel couldn't pinpoint the cause of her discomfort, a feeling she later recognized as anxiety. To her dismay, she started to feel anxious more often as she returned to school in the fall.

She noticed herself associating anxiety with specific events. Soon she was avoiding anything taking place outside, involving large crowds, or people who were intoxicated. Putting this all together, Rachel realized her fear centered around vomit. She was terrified of throwing up or being around others who were vomiting. Although this isn't an activity people generally look forward to, she became utterly consumed by the need to avoid it. If she could control it at all, she would never get sick, and she would never be around someone who was.

Among other self-imposed restrictions, she stopped eating what she called "danger foods." These started with shrimp, undercooked foods, and cookie dough, but she eventually resorted to only eating bread because its absorption qualities made her feel safe. Despite her previously full life on campus, surrounded by those she loved and loved to care for, Rachel "fell off the face of the Earth that semester." She declined invitations to events on campus and drove over 30 minutes home to her parents every day after class. Rachel felt afraid every day and relied heavily on her parents during this time. Her life felt empty.

One day, Rachel decided enough was enough. She knew something needed to change, living with these strict self-imposed limits was not her "God-intended purpose." She sought help from the mental health resources on campus, where she was assessed and given the names of a few local therapists. This first step felt bold, as she never saw herself as someone who would have a mental health issue. She previously believed mental health was something she could just "tough" her way through. But she realized if she wanted to get better, it was her responsibility to find a therapist and stick with them.

For Rachel, acknowledging something was wrong and asking for help was significant and bold. She reached out to a therapist who specializes in phobias and began imitation therapy sessions. During visits, Rachel sat in the therapist's office with her eyes closed as the therapist described scenarios that would most trigger her anxiety. The goal was to work on different distraction techniques to relax once she was in the cycle of peak anxiety. Rachel chose to also take medication, which ironically had potential side effects of nausea.

The activities that generated the most fear for Rachel included being a designated driver, attending concerts, riding public transportation, and riding in the car as a passenger instead of the driver. All these activities put her in scenarios where she didn't feel in control. Recognizing control as a larger challenge allowed her faith to step in. Rachel's personal relationship with

God helped her to trust she would be alright even when she leaves her comfort zone. She reminds herself, "God has my back and my best interest in mind - even if it involves someone throwing up on me." With her faith in mind, Rachel slowly started saying yes to things where she knew she would have to give up control. As she started to have more positive experiences with these activities, utilizing her newfound distraction techniques, the activities started to become decreasingly scary. Each time, the decision felt momentous, whether it was accepting when a friend offered to drive or going on a spring break trip with a large group of college students. She was afraid to make these choices, but knew they were necessary to lead the life she wanted. Today, Rachel recognizes boldness in her everyday choices like riding in the backseat of a car for an hour-long road trip or drinking two alcoholic beverages in a night rather than one.

Now that she lives in a new city, Rachel hasn't shared this part of her life with many people. She doesn't want this story to get in the way of how she lives now. She explains, "if people don't know, they won't treat me differently. They won't adjust to make it easier for me. I'm forced to be okay enough and swallow my fear, which is good. It's the only path forward. I can handle this and have proven it to myself repeatedly." Although she is more comfortable in the scenarios she previously worked so hard to avoid, she still catches herself creating limits and calculated decisions. When she is around friends who are drinking alcohol, she will keep tabs on how much everyone has consumed, so she can better avoid those becoming the most drunk. She is still terrified of being a designated driver and will make excuses whenever possible to leave early and drive herself home or to walk, because doing so feels less risky. The act of sharing her story with me for this book, when so few people here are aware of this part of her life, is bold.

Rachel's definition of bold was turned on its head. No longer did boldness have to be something like being the first person to accomplish a new feat. Boldness could be something seemingly smaller, or at least more repeatable. She could make several different bold choices in one week. When her weeks feel the fullest, or most normal, they likely had many bold decisions along the way. In her words, "living life is bold and everyone severely underestimates their personal boldness." I now completely agree. Most of my interviewees initially claimed they didn't find themselves as bold. Some people are underestimating themselves, but not every life is one filled with boldness. So, I encourage you to choose boldness in your life, and recognize when you already have chosen it.

What is one thing you can say yes to, when you might initially be afraid? What's one area where you can opt to relinquish control?

Self-worth

One of the many things we can't control are our friendships. Although we can heavily influence them, we are never the only ones making them work. They are a two-way street, and that can either be relieving or infuriating, depending on how the friendship is going. Or sometimes, it can just be sad. Not all friendships grow or even stay the same.

One of my friends and inspirations, Hannah, is kind, outdoorsy, and fun. We met in the context of work and immediately connected on running and faith. She was assigned to the Chicago site for our summer internship, and I was assigned to Charlotte. I had never been to Chicago, so when we found out our company would cover the entry fee to the Rock 'n' Roll Half Marathon, I went and stayed with her for the weekend. She was a great tour guide, and we ran side by side for the first ten miles of the race, which was the longest I had ever run next to someone. In all my long runs, I had never matched someone else's pace for that long. After the weekend, we started a habit of Face Timing every few months. We have always lived multiple states away from each other but keep as close as we can.

Three years later, I visited Hannah in Idaho for a week and a half of hiking and river swimming. We encountered more wildlife than anticipated and in a throwback to elementary school music class, she played a recorder to scare a moose away from us on the trail. "I find that playing music at it is more respectful than yelling at it." The next day, when we had started talking about boldness, we discovered multiple fresh sets of grizzly bear tracks on our trail. We paused for a few minutes debating what our plan of action should be, whether to forge ahead the additional 4.5 miles to our campsite or turn around to the car. We wanted to be safe but didn't know if continuing to the campsite would lead to a bear sighting. I had spent months telling people why boldness mattered to me and didn't want to take the easy route if we felt safe enough with our circumstances. But as we discussed our options, we agreed sticking it out would not be wise, so we turned around to the car. (Mom, are you proud?)

We drove to Yellowstone Lake and Hannah continued her thoughts on boldness until we were interrupted by an alarmingly close Bison and hit the road once again. Hannah's story was different than any I had heard so far, culminating not around one action, but a change in mindset. Initially, I asked her questions I had asked most of my interviewees, hoping to fit her story into the formulaic mold I had grown comfortable writing. That kind of expectation for her story limited her experience and the possibilities of boldness.

Hannah graduated from Miami Ohio, and moved to a small town in New Hampshire, living in a house that didn't have cell service or WIFI. She had said final goodbyes to some classmates, but had hoped to stay in touch with her friends and family despite the long-distance. This new home without cell coverage put a big damper on those plans. How could she keep up if she couldn't call them regularly? She went from living with her best friends and spending time with them daily to not knowing when she could interact with them next. That was a drastic change for Hannah.

Hannah found herself in low spirits for her first several months in New Hampshire, thinking she was just homesick. The longer that feeling persisted, the more she thought about what she was missing. She lived close to family friends and her childhood hometown, so she eventually concluded that, "I feel at home here, I can't blame this on homesickness anymore. This is something that's deeper than where in the world I am, and this is something that will follow me unless I work on it."

She had always enjoyed caring for her loved ones with words of encouragement, hosting them for meals, giving them rides, or finding any other way to serve them. "I've always loved taking care of people... Service, whether it's a person you know really well or a stranger, is one of the best ways to build community. It's like saying "I'm next to you... whatever we're going through." When she was distant from many of her closest family and friends, she felt like she didn't have a feasible way to serve them. She feared, "If I couldn't take care of those people, they wouldn't know how much I loved them, and they wouldn't want to spend time with me anymore because they didn't feel cared for." Would they still want to be her friend, or would these relationships fade to the background? Identifying these fears helped her realize what was at the root of her recent despair and emptiness. "I had been basing my self-worth on how well I could take care of the people I loved," and that placement of her identity was "self-deprecating and harmful... mentally, emotionally, and spiritually."

Acknowledging and accepting she needed to alter her mindset was the first portion of this story where Hannah felt bold. "I'm never really going to have joy if I'm limiting the way I feel about my place in the world around all this." She knew she needed to recenter her identity and self-worth onto something less limiting, something that wouldn't leave her empty when she didn't have the opportunity to excel. Since then, she has been working towards returning her identity to her Christian faith.

Beyond recognizing the need for a major mindset shift, Hannah felt bold "allowing myself to grieve and mourn those friendships or those things I felt were changing and then choose joy in every moment anyway." This may be a new concept for some readers, grieving a friendship even though it may continue in some capacity going forward. The grieving comes in knowing from now on it will be different. The night of my graduation, I said goodbye to James and Jake, whom you have read about. All three of us were moving to different states, and I didn't know when I would see them again. I knew we would stay friends to some extent, but no matter how hard I tried, it would never be the same as living daily life with them. That was heartbreaking, and I couldn't help but feel sad.

Like me, after graduating, Hannah let herself get upset and grieve the end of that time in her life. She had said goodbye to friends before, but this was in a much larger magnitude. This was a goodbye to everyone all at once, at a time when her identity was wrapped around her ability to care for them. "It had never been tied to self-worth... until the transition of leaving college." She had to mourn her friendships as she knew them and her identity as she had known it. She had to feel her emotions instead of bottling them up to make room for a choice of joy. "You can have great joy because of things you experience with somebody and appreciate it

for what it was and accept it has ended." Hannah also found
moments of joy by being present with her friends.

Hannah was also intentional in the months afterwards
when she experienced sadness or missed her friends. "It's hard to
admit sometimes when you miss somebody. It's hard to call
somebody and say, "I really miss you and it's hard to be far away
from you," especially if the other person isn't mourning or grieving
the transition in the same way.

This shift in mindset and identity hasn't been instant.
"Figuring out how to think about myself separate from others was
weird and still is weird... growth is not linear." Hannah has been
processing and trying a few different things to set herself up for
success. "My phone background is usually a Bible verse or a phrase
I have found to be grounding. Right now, it says 'pace yourself,
pace yourself, pace yourself.' Something I found really benefited
me in this process is allowing myself to rest and reboot, asking for
help when I need to be cared for." She has started to recognize
when she cares for herself, she can better position herself to be
more present and more invested when she's with others. She has
become more "protective of things that are more restorative vs.
things that take a lot of energy." Hannah checks her motives when
she adds more things onto her plate, asking herself, "am I doing
this out of love or am I doing this out of fear, that if I don't show
up to this, will they think I don't care?" She has been looking for
ways other than service to extend her love to the people she cares
about, so she can protect her energy levels and prevent herself
from falling into her old, limiting self-identity.

Hannah's story was the first example I heard of boldness that didn't culminate around a specific action. She felt bold shifting her mindset and perspective, while staying where she was. That took a while for me to wrap my head around because it didn't fit neatly into my formula. In all my interviews, I had asked for the context, the bold action, and the impact of the action. But as she was speaking, I knew this, too, was an example of boldness. She challenged herself, risking pain, acknowledged the friendships that might fade away, and stripped herself of her source of self-worth.

When have you embraced a transition for what it was, saying good-bye to how things were before?

God Laughs

We make plans for a reason. We want to be prepared; we want things to go smoothly. We can plan better for ourselves, more than anyone else can, right? But our plans don't always come to fruition. This is a reality that Cameron, Cam for short, knows all too well.

Cameron is a pilot for the United States Air Force, which I find extremely impressive. He works intensely hard, but I would say he is only serious or stern when he must be. Don't tell his superiors, but to me, he's the guy with an endless stream of SpongeBob references. He's a home-grown country boy who has muscadines growing in his backyard. One of my favorite memories with Cam was when we rode in the car with our feet out the window, driving back from the lake, blasting 'Living the Dream'.

We met the first weekend of college and we have watched each other grow up quite a bit since then. Our friendship reached a unique level for a time because we dated siblings of the same family, gathering for family dinners and double dates all in one. We have always connected over our faith, and he got me into my favorite book: Love Does by Bob Goff.

Cam's bold story is a little unique - it doesn't culminate around one decision or one action point. It's a pattern. In a series of circumstances, Cam continues to make the same choice. Let me explain.

Cam was single during our senior year of college, and with his plan to join the Air Force after graduation, he thought, "I'm done dating for a while, and I'll worry about it later." This is the first time Cam felt "God was almost laughing at the plans I had," because he went home for winter break and ran into Annie. He planned to just go on a date or two, "I'm just doing this to pass the time over Christmas break." But on their third date, they "really clicked" and he started to realize Annie "might be more than just trying to pass the time over Christmas break." They continued dating and I remember Cam considering marrying Annie as early as that March. But he was still planning to leave in May to begin pilot training, and who knew what might happen to their relationship? Annie was "hesitant to keep dating, knowing he was leaving." It was risky.

In this circumstance, Cam trusted God. Unlike Cam, God knew what He was doing. After graduation, Cam's training date was delayed several months, giving him more time to stay in town, continuing to date Annie. After that, his training date was delayed again. In total, it was pushed back about a year from the original schedule. "It was huge." Here, Cam recognized God's plan was "1000 times better than I could have imagined it." While these delays gave them extra time, Cam was still set to leave for Texas. Even so, they continued to date until a week before he left. Without discussing or seeking validation from anyone, even his parents, Cam proposed to Annie.

Soon they started the wedding plans; it was going to be perfect. It would take place over Memorial Day weekend, when he had an opportunity to leave base and go back home. But when they were a few months out, they started to worry it might not be able to happen. There started to be more and more restrictions as the COVID-19 pandemic picked up speed. The dates for when Cam would be allowed to leave base got pushed back, then pushed back again. "I tried doing everything on my own again... It didn't feel like He was helping me at all." Cam felt like he was losing control of everything. He was "locked down in Texas" without the ability to leave or to take leave. "All the wedding plans went out the window."

They prayed about it, accepted their circumstance, and trusted God. Then, Annie moved out to join Cam in Del Rio, Texas. She sacrificed all the "glamorous" parts of her originally planned celebration, choosing instead to get married however they could, in the middle of their living room. They didn't have the fanfare or family members in attendance they had dreamed of, but they had each other.

Turns out this was better for them than trying to wait and have a 'normal' wedding. Getting married when they did blessed them with more quality time than they could have ever anticipated. Annie found a job she loved, and Cam was placed into a day job with predictable hours while he waited an additional four months for pilot training to begin. The Lord provided the quality time "a newlywed couple needs," compared to what they would have planned for themselves; the difference was stark. "If we would have waited, or even if the pilot training would have been at the normal timing, I would be studying like crazy, and we wouldn't have gotten that quality time...God laughs at our plans... He's totally in control." Trusting God, not knowing what the future would hold, required boldness from both Cam and Annie and it was worth it.

Fast forwarding to Cam's completion of flight training, Cam thought he knew what would be best for their family going forward. He would do his best to get a plane assignment that had a stereotype for being grounded often, a tanker, increasing his chances of being home. But when he got the list of available planes, there was only one tanker listed. He had less than three hours to talk with Annie and submit his preferences, not having a clue how to rank the remainder of the list. They prayed God would "send us where we can do the most work for you and we will be happy." They trusted God wouldn't give them anything they couldn't handle. They surrendered their future home to someone outside of themselves. This act of surrender fits in well with a quote by author Charles Feltman, "Trust is choosing to risk making something you value vulnerable to another person's actions.[2]"

At the big assignment reveal, someone else got the tanker. Cam was placed with his fourth choice. It was a C-17, based in Hawaii. "Dream come true, getting to live in Hawaii, but what the heck?!... never got our hopes up for that one because everyone wants to go to Hawaii... didn't think it was possible." They hadn't initially ranked it as their top choice because it was known to be a very time-consuming assignment and he wouldn't have as much time at home. But now they looked forward to their future move to Hawaii, excited and doing their best to trust in God's plan instead of trying to "control every detail."

Cam describes his learnings with a hypothetical: "if God threw a wrench in my plan, I'm going to stay positive... Not trying to make it work how I want it to." It is not Cam's natural inclination to do this; it's hard for him. Not knowing what the future holds, Cam often gets his hopes set on specific details, thinking he knows what will be best for his life. "I thought my plan was right because I made it." Submitting can feel scary, because it relinquishes control. By trusting in God, Cam aims to stop his habit of editing and salvaging as much of his original plan as possible, and to instead "let go completely".

---

[2] *Feltman, Charles, et al. The Thin Book of Trust: An Essential Primer for Building Trust at Work. Unspecified, 2009.*

When Cam is ultimately confronted by the realization of God's plan instead of his own, he's humbled. He thinks he "should have learned by now" but finds himself making the same attempt to control the details of his life. Over the last several years, Cam has become increasingly aware of his pattern of plan-making. "As humans we try to become more and more controlling; He calls us back to him." Despite the pattern, it is not the same thing each time. His learnings require increasingly less time to process, because "every time it happens, it becomes easier and easier to recognize it." Cam continues to learn and adjust his mindset when he is faced with an unforeseen scenario.

In Cam's opportunity to date during his senior year of college, in the specifics of his wedding, and in his plane assignment, Cam found boldness. In those circumstances, events didn't progress as he had expected or even hoped for. In those moments, he confidently chose to trust God, not knowing what would come next. This isn't the first time his plan was trumped by God's, and it certainly won't be the last. His choice to trust could come across as a passive one, but in reality, it was the assumption of great risk. Boldness doesn't always require action. Sometimes the boldest thing you can do is to embrace what cards you've been dealt.

When did all of your plans change due to something outside of your control? How did you react?

Competition and Comparison

Success means different things to different people. To control our possibility of success, we can always work harder. Persistence can bring you most of the way, but sometimes there is an element of chance. Will opportunities become available at the right time? Holding on to self-imposed deadlines can leave us exhausted and discouraged by our progress.

My friend Kat experienced multiple iterations of defining what success meant to her. She is one of my closest friends from college. She is incredibly loyal and supportive, enthusiastically and proudly hyping her friends up for their aspirations and accomplishments. She is always ready for an adventure, bear hug, or dance party. She's one of my favorite people and I love we currently call the same city home.

Like many other students at UNC Chapel Hill, Kat started her freshman year as a biology major. She was on a pre-medical school path, which put her in challenging courses often called "weed-out" classes due to the number of students who change majors after taking them. The students in these classes are extremely focused on their grades, hoping their performance in school will be enough. Not only do they have to do well, but they must also perform better than their peers in order to earn acceptance into a medical school. Grades depended primarily on a couple tests scored by bell curves. This competitive field bred major feelings of self-comparison for Kat.

Kat would spend countless hours studying. When I realized the only time I could spend with her was in the library, I showed up, watching movies like Tarzan, on my computer. While I was enjoying feel-good films, Kat was feeling loads of pressure. These were hardly just tests for her; Kat felt her self-worth and emotional state depended on her performance. Good grades evoked pride, accomplishment, and celebration, while bad grades felt like personal failures. With her emotional well-being tied to performance throughout undergrad, she "felt very stuck".

Kat kept toughing it out because she wanted to succeed. She saw success in a couple different options: medical school and Physician Assistant (PA) school. If she didn't get into either of those options, she would have failed herself – "there was no wiggle room." As many college seniors are familiar, many of Kat's family and friends started to ask her about her post-college plans, and each time she found herself speaking about PA school, she felt as though she was "being validated in only one path." After graduating, she worked at a medical practice with several other PA school hopefuls. This environment, like school, bred more competition and calculations of "how you measure up." She describes the whole endeavor as "so unnecessarily competitive... if you get in, you succeed, if you don't, you fail."

Kat understood the competitive aspect and feeling of needing to prove herself would not end once she got into school. She started to realize this lifestyle was not something she wanted to keep up with. She had now spent five years dedicated to science and a career in healthcare, but found herself asking the question, "what else is there?" She stumbled on the idea of public health, and "felt like I needed to apply" to a master's program at UNC.

She took the opportunity, despite it being different from what she had initially been looking for.

The hard and scary part for Kat was when she started bringing the idea up in conversations with family and friends. She talked about it as a steppingstone before eventually going to PA school as originally intended, not wanting to change the goal she had been pursuing for so long. Switching gears entirely would mean several things, less need for her previous biology expertise, "a pay cut, and a job that's not as well understood." The US emphasizes and allocates resources towards treating sick people, not leaving as much towards prevention. The public health and prevention spaces aren't as well understood, and this applies to the titles given to their professionals as well. Generally, people recognize titles like M.D. more than they do titles like M.P.H., Master of Public Health.

Once she started the public health program, she "felt relieved and passionate about the material," sensing the intense pressure of the last several years was no longer part of her journey now. Throughout her first semester, however, she would tell others if she got into PA school, she would drop out of her current program to pursue it. It took her a while to commit to her new journey because it "hurt to give up on something she had been working towards." Kat described it as a loss of "the life I thought I was going to have. I was mourning that for a bit."

Eventually, Kat "realized she loved this program, and this is what she wants to do." She started to tell others about her interest in pursuing public health instead of using it as a steppingstone. That change in mindset and willingness to speak of it honestly with people she cared about was a bold transition for Kat. She was nervous to tell her parents she wanted to stay in public health instead of eventually switching out. She was scared to tell other mentors who knew what her initial aspirations were. She was afraid because they might perceive her change in goals as a failure. But she boldly stepped past those fears and discomfort, coming forward with her new plan. Fortunately, no one doubted her or asked, "are you sure?"

In all, Kat experienced "ridiculous sunk costs" from time spent studying for the GRE, shadowing, and majoring in biology. All of that could have been spent other ways, like taking a social dance class with me and our other friends. That is the part that hurts her the most – "why did I lose so much time?" While it pains her to lose progress, she knows it's worth it to pursue her new path.

Choosing her current path ultimately felt freeing for Kat. "Finding that freedom has made me feel so much more peace about any future big decisions." Already, it has impacted how she approaches application interviews. She felt freedom to choose internships because she was genuinely interested in the work, not because of its status like she would have previously done. Now Kat pursues things, "because I want to, not because I feel like I have to."

Kat's boldness came in speaking up and committing to her decision more than it did in making the decision itself. When have you taken ownership of something that might not be well-received or well-understood by others? Was it a focus of study, an idea, a dream, or another part of yourself?

Divine Detour

In a culture that craves efficiency, indirect routes can be the enemy. Whether we're driving or planning our careers, we want to know which direction we're going. We can often search for the most linear path, avoiding turns if at all possible. But in real life, we don't know what is around the next curve or what will happen next. Do we really need to know the next stop along the journey before we walk out the door? To be an efficient navigator, maybe. But to arrive eventually, perhaps not. My friend Molly had carefully set goals, but when she found herself working towards something new, she embraced the unknown and kept going.

Molly is six feet of joy. She is one of the sweet girls I met while I lived in California. She shared with me details of life as an actor and lives an example of what it looks like to fully trust God. She is welcoming, says what she feels, and regularly quotes fun phrases like "holy smokes!" Molly is also known to improvise her own lyrics to songs instead of looking them up, which cracks me up.

For most of her life, Molly wanted to be a musical theater performer. She is "incredibly passionate about the theater industry and people coming to know Jesus through the theater industry." It's one of the things I associate with her: Molly is an actor. But for various reasons, including opportunity, this has been "put on pause." Acknowledging she had a period where she would be taking a break from performing; she prayed, asking how she should use her time instead. Molly felt there was a clear answer to that prayer. "God so tangibly said, 'you need to go back to school.'" She had never considered additional schooling as an option. She was the "last person anyone would have guessed to go back to school," because she was so sure of her path as an actor. But suddenly, she had a desire to go back to school to learn more about Jesus. It didn't make any sense. Why did she want this all of a sudden?

Surprised by this clear and specific desire that was so different from her previous plans, she sought out support from friends. In one of those conversations, Molly was asked what she wanted to be when she was a child. After some contemplation, Molly remembered she had once written in her journal: "I want to be the next female Billy Graham." When her friend indicated Molly's childhood goal was both a unique desire and related to the field of study Molly was now considering, things started to click. Molly felt a sense of peace about this shift in interests, realizing for her, God "brought a childhood passion back into my adult life… He knows these secret desires of our hearts even if we have forgotten them."

The scary part for Molly was not knowing what would come next. In comparison to the theater industry which she understood so well, going back to school brought with it many unknown possibilities. "Everything was up in the air," and it was scary. "My boldness was responding to the unknown and stepping out in faith." Molly found her courage and her confidence, "trusting that I serve a good and a gracious Father who wants my best interests."

Molly boldly applied to a graduate program at Biola University and was accepted. Since then, "God has affirmed in so many incredible ways this is exactly where I need to be." Through her mindset and attention to her faith at Biola, she found herself in a massive period of growth. "God's unlocking all these different capacities and passions in my heart." She has been able to recognize more of her natural tendencies and some misunderstandings in how she had previously viewed God's character. Now, she's "not in a posture of viewing God as a genie," like she had most of her life. Now she views Him more as a friend to spend time with beyond making requests or asking favors.

Even once she had started her program, this shift in career path created an opportunity for Molly to question herself. For so long, her hope was in her future success in musical theater. But in the 'storms of life,' that version of success felt lost. "Culture tells us what success is and it's bold to go against that." Molly is still learning what success looks like for her now and chooses to move her identity from her career to "something that's unmovable," Christ. It doesn't mean she no longer wants success in her career, or she doesn't care about it. "It doesn't mean I'm never going to perform again." She may find opportunities to embrace her love for performing again in the future. She has no idea of what is to come. She calls this season in her life her "divine detour" and feels peace not knowing where she will end up, because the "best part of road trips are the pit stops, not this great destination." In her everyday life, Molly's confidence comes from believing "our 'partner-in-crime' next to us is the God of the universe – we can't fail even if culture says that we have."

Through this process, Molly has been reminded she is not in control of everything in her life. She is glad this is the case, because often her circumstances work out better for her than if everything went the way she wanted it to. Recognizing her lack of control forces her to trust in God, instead of her own effort, even when it's challenging. Even when it involves loss of identity or otherwise. "If everything is peachy keen, sometimes we feel like we don't have a need for God." Trusting in God and making decisions based on that trust, despite the unknown, was where Molly found her boldness. "Stepping out in boldness ain't easy. It's hard, but you have to be willing to get your hands dirty." Molly found the reward is worth the risk. "It's so wonderful to see the fruit of stepping out in boldness... sometimes we don't see the results... but that shouldn't stop us from being bold."

Not all of my readers are likely to believe in and trust in God to guide their path. Where do you find courage to step forward, even when you have no idea what is coming next?

<u>5</u>

Vulnerability

One of the most rewarding aspects of being human is interactions with others. Our interactions and relationships can bring us a sense of meaning, acceptance, pleasure, and community. But it's not always easy. We want to belong, we want to be chosen, whether romantically or platonically. In order to find ourselves in that position, we often need to put ourselves out there. But it's often scary – putting ourselves out there risks possible rejection.

What if this stranger doesn't want to be my friend? What if my friendship will be ruined when I'm honest with my friend about how their actions hurt me? What if it's too late, and they won't forgive me? What if they don't like me? What if I end this relationship and don't find another one that's better? These 'what ifs' plague us and can prevent us from true and full connections. If you don't give them the option to be your friend, they don't have the option to reject you, but you also lose the connection. If you aren't honest with your friends about how they make you feel, you sacrifice intimacy and the quality of the connection. If you don't apologize, the chances of reconciliation are slimmer. If you don't ask, you could wait a lifetime for your answer.

We all want to be fully known and fully loved. Yet we find it incredibly challenging to open up, to tell our friends and family what's really going on in our lives. How we have been hurt, what we're really looking forward to, what they mean to us, how we have messed up, the list goes on. Why is it so hard? Where did these emotional walls come from? Have we been hurt before? Perhaps it's a fear if we get to the point where we are fully known, we still won't be accepted by those we love the most. That sounds terrifying enough to me.

The next stories show examples of people who have knocked their walls down to start, change, mend, or end a relationship with another human being. They have let others in, exposing their raw and real selves. Doing this puts them at risk and releases any control of the relationship they had previously. It is all up to their newfound confidant to respond to their vulnerability either in acceptance and grace or rejection. These stories will take you through their choice to boldly embrace vulnerability and how it impacted their relationships afterwards.

Blindsided Best Friend

This story is another from my personal life. If I were only allowed to include one story to answer my own question, "When have you been the boldest in your life?" this would be it. So, buckle up, because this one's a doozy!

The spring semester of my junior year of college, I spent almost all my free time with my best friend, who I'll call Hunter. We would toss frisbees in the quad, ride bikes, attend church together, and talk about anything and everything. I loved spending time with him - he was different from everyone else. He was shameless, often acting like an absolute goon. He was loud and talked in a language all his own, intentionally throwing vowels incorrectly, putting emphasis on specific consonants for no apparent reason. He was a die-hard Browns fan, because for some reason he enjoyed wearing clashing colors and being grumpy every Sunday. Hunter was so many things, but most importantly, he was my best friend in the world.

For a long time, I knew I had 'caught feelings' for Hunter. I tried to shove the feelings deep down for a while, because I knew Hunter was the type of person who would pursue if he felt attraction towards someone. He hadn't ever tried anything romantic with me, so I held onto what I did have: friendship. I tried to reason with myself I couldn't possibly like this clown I called my best friend, because he was simply too ridiculous. Apparently, my logic wasn't convincing enough to change my own mind, since the feelings only grew. I knew bottling up my feelings wasn't healthy, so I told a few people I trusted. My housemates that year heard his name come up a plethora of times. It was easy to talk about my feelings with others, it wasn't risky. The real risk would come only if I were to tell Hunter.

My friendship predicament soon proved painful, and increasingly unbearable. He would do things that stood out from my other guy friends, which made me so confused. He showed up out of the blue at my door, having baked me cheesecake for Valentine's Day. Another time, we went on a 15-mile bike ride and then to the lake, which we agreed felt very much like a date activity. That day, we talked about what we each hoped for in our future relationships and marriages, and I couldn't help but think I seemed to fit everything he was looking for. When he asked what I was looking for, I did my best not to describe him to a tee. As we sat side-by-side on the beach of the lake that afternoon, my thoughts were swirling about him until he interrupted the chaos with a question. He asked for help responding to a random girl on Tinder.

Can we take a collective deep breath for younger me? Ouch... that question hurt. The stab of rejection proved he would much rather seek out a stranger than consider dating me. But he must have considered it at some point, right? Surely, at least one person had asked him why he was spending so much time with me, whether there was something more than friendship between us. Considered or not, his request for romantic advice validated my fears. Guess I made the right call by hiding my feelings from him.

How could I possibly give him a response without blowing my cover? I don't remember exactly what I said, but I tried my best to brush it off. Either I was a talented actor, or he was blissfully blind, because he didn't notice anything was up. But I couldn't keep up the charade for much longer, it was too painful. Something needed to change, because I couldn't bear to continue our friendship the way it was. I couldn't harbor feelings while spending most of my waking hours with him. I couldn't handle it if he kept talking about other girls.

I told our close mutual friend James (see page 47) how I felt about Hunter. I knew he would only last a couple days before he broke the news to Hunter. It was too big, and they were too close for him to sit on that information. My time clock had started - I needed to work up the courage to tell Hunter before James did.

But I still almost didn't tell him. It was the day before I left for a trip, and we had, like so many days before, spent the entire day together. I was dropping him off in the evening, and still hadn't told him. I pulled into his driveway, and he was about to get out when I said, "I need to tell you something." He skeptically said "okayyy," and my heart was beating a thousand times a minute. I took a deep breath and kept my hands on the wheel to stop them from shaking. Then with every ounce of courage I could muster, I told Hunter I really liked him, and I couldn't continue to be friends the way we were. I wasn't particularly asking him to date me, but if he wasn't interested, I needed space. I couldn't be the first person he turned to, his choice of comfort, celebration, and advice, unless we were in a relationship.

Blindsided, he asked for time to think before he responded. We went an entire week without communicating. I tried to enjoy my week at the beach, but thoughts of his potential response weighed upon my mind. I knew he cared about me but questioned how much. He knew me more deeply than others did - would he possibly choose me after all? I was now vulnerable, waiting on his verdict. If anyone was going to want me, wouldn't it be him?

When I returned, he confirmed the suspicion I had held for so long, he didn't see me romantically. My best friend had officially friend-zoned me. Only now, upon my request, our friendship would be shrinking, too. Was space really what I wanted?

The next morning, before 6am, I was in the airport for another trip. Thank God, I had another distraction. Even when I was back in North Carolina, I only saw him a couple more times that summer. Our almost constant interactions were now limited to infrequent phone calls. It was heart-breaking to feel like I had completely lost him, but the space was necessary. Alone, I had a chance to process and move forward with a clear mind. I eventually got over Hunter - I didn't continue to pine after him from afar. He no longer had power over me in the way he used to.

But to this day, I'm still fearful I might be friend-zoned by someone else in the future. A high percentage of my friends has always been male due to my hobbies, but I don't want to be 'one of the guys.' When I'm specifically interested in someone, I don't want to be passive, afraid to flirt. I would rather face early rejection than repeat a possible blindside situation like with Hunter.

I still call Hunter my friend, but this friendship is nowhere like it had been previously. Ultimately, losing my best friend was the hardest thing to come to terms with, not the rejection. I miss him. We still talk every few months, but I'm guarded with him now. I'm not typically one to put up boundaries, but with Hunter, they are necessary. It still saddens me when I think about how much we have lost. When you enjoy spending time with someone, you typically want more time together, not less. It's so frustrating and incomprehensible I enjoyed spending time with him so much I had to say goodbye.

The only advice I've gotten from both married couples and romantic comedies alike is you should fall for your best friend. What they don't give advice on is when you do, but it's not reciprocated. What then?

Even if I did believe in regrets, I wouldn't ever regret this bold moment. The downfalls of my bold choice to tell Hunter how I felt about him are the most tangible, yet the rewards exist as well. I was able to remove myself from an increasingly painful situation and set boundaries - which is incredibly hard for me to do. I am proud of myself for actually telling him, when it would have been easy to slowly stop communicating, leaving him clueless as to why I no longer wanted to spend time with him. In hindsight, telling him was the scariest thing I have ever chosen to do. This was the boldest I've ever been. Having accomplished it, I know I can do other scary things when they come up.

When have you made yourself vulnerable to the opinion or choice of someone else?

Gentle Kindness

Telling someone what they mean to you can be scary when it's platonic, too. Seriously communicating how much you value or appreciate someone can change the nature of your friendship going forward. Especially with guys, affection isn't always commonly or clearly portrayed among friends. When affection is given, it might feel uncomfortable and unsolicited although well-intentioned. Matt W. has experienced varying levels of appreciation and vulnerability in his friendships and found it can be challenging to bring specific friendships from one level to another.

Matt is one of my great friends from college. He's a goofball, loves dabbing far more than the average person, and shares my love of Jesus and Thomas Rhett. He is a deep thinker and great listener, and since he was a rare English major at school, he was the first person I asked for advice when I had the idea to write a book. Matt is now in seminary school, where he reads and writes more than he ever has before. He has a mind from which I can continually learn.

Despite his affectionate bromance with his college roommate, he has told me communicating his appreciation and love towards anyone other than his wife, Susan, doesn't feel natural. In fact, when one of his closest guy friends, during freshman year, said he loved Matt, all Matt could do was stare at him and say "okay." Looking back, he calls that a moment of weakness, not appropriately responding to his more emotionally mature friend. He was really thrown off by it because he had previously never heard the words "I love you" from a guy friend. His choice to respond with "okay," was not because he didn't reciprocate that same sentiment towards his friend, but because he was fearful. Matt's fear was not that others would overhear him, but a fear of expressing any kind of affection. "Oh, I can't say that. It would be weird." Regardless of Matt's fear, he found his friend's verbal expression of affection progressed and defined their relationship.

Fast forward to Matt's senior year of college, when he lived in a house of six men who regularly roasted and teased each other. Roasting is a common way of friends playfully making fun of each other and calling them out. One housemate enjoyed it more than the rest, and worked insults into conversations frequently, even upon greeting. Instead of a typical greeting like, "Hey Matt, how are you?" he would opt for the harsher, "Hey Matt, you're a bitch." As with many guy friends, this was the understood standard of humor, not unfamiliar to the dynamic of the house. His housemate, Greg, would roast others in similar ways, and said roasting was how he showed affection. If he roasted you, it was because he liked you. For a while, Matt would attempt to match Greg in this style. He would try to roast Greg back.

One day in Matt's personal Bible reading, he came across Proverbs 15:1, "A gentle answer turns away wrath, but a harsh word stirs up anger." He took this message's application to his life as an opportunity to respond to Greg in gentle kindness. Combined with another verse Romans 16:16, "Greet each other with a holy kiss," he thought about this intentionally. Changing his dynamic with Greg risked making each of them uncomfortable and being immediately shot down with an additional insult thrown in his face. He was fearful of rejection, but boldly chose to overcome that risk, because previously he had been given an opportunity to express his affection for his friend and regretted not taking it. With this decided, Matt waited for another standard greeting from Greg. Greg walked past him with the usual line, "Hey Matt, you're a bitch." Matt swallowed his pride, took the insult, and responded with love saying, "Hey Greg, I love you." Greg literally stopped in his tracks, with a look of shock. His face displayed his confusion, his natural rhythm abruptly coming to a halt, likely never hearing a response like that from anyone else.

While Matt never spoke to his friends in this way growing up, it turned into a pattern. Eventually, Greg would add onto the pattern, responding with "I love you, too." It became part of their dynamic. Greg insulted him often, and now they end up saying the three words, "I love you", just as often. For them, the frequency of the phrase didn't equate to any loss in significance. Each time they say it genuinely, they positively impact their friendship in a way both can tangibly recognize. This friendly affection started with Greg, and now Matt expresses it with another close friend. While Matt can see the success of friendly affection in his relationship with Greg, it is still risky for each additional friend he brings over that emotional hump. The first time he changes the dynamic of any friendship by inserting words of affirmation instead of roasting, it feels bold. It seems to me Matt has found himself a repeatable opportunity to choose boldness over fear.

Recently, Matt spent several hours with a group of male college students who roasted each other continually for the duration of the gathering. "It's just how they have fun together. It reminded me of my experience in college." Looking from the outside in, Matt wondered if they too, feel an uneasiness from the roasting, on edge as though they must consistently perform. One slip up, and they will be greeted by a friend, but not a sensitive or grace-filled one. For most of his life, Matt's standard was roasting. He did find it funny, but also discovered a difference in how he would share personal details with friends based on whether they participated in roasting or not. When he had bad days, he would be much less likely to turn to a friend who regularly roasted him. In his vulnerable moments, he would turn towards the friends who didn't participate in roasting. He didn't trust friends like Greg to refrain from an opportunity to make fun of him when he really needed support and grace. Indirectly, the roasting interactions limited the closeness of his friendships with those individuals, limiting the safe space to talk. Perhaps this prevents many, like Matt, from creating habits of vulnerability and affection with their pals.

In the future, Matt no longer wants to relate to his friends through roasting, insulting, or sarcasm. While some choose to love on friends by adding kind words, he sees power in refusing to roast, reducing the unkind words. When we intentionally look for ways to love our friends, we can go about it in a plethora of ways. In addition to verbal affirmation, we can choose to physically hug our friends. Matt says, "Physical and verbal affection feels identical for me, and I want more of my friendships to require hugs."

I find it incredibly interesting that Matt chose to be represented by this story. Personally, I have never felt comfortable with roasting. When I'm with friends who tend to roast each other, I'm constantly afraid I will end up the butt of one of the jokes and I might not be able to handle it. I have always thought that said more about my personal sensitivity than it did about roasting, but now I'm not so sure. Yes, I am likely more sensitive to teasing than others, but this meaningful conversation with Matt makes me wonder how many others feel a similar need to perform around their roasting friends instead of being their authentic selves?

Perhaps roasting isn't a regular part of your dynamic, but you still feel uncomfortable expressing your affection and appreciation of your friends. How can you challenge yourself to let your close and trusted friends know how you feel about them?

Keep a Smile

Next, I will share a story about a friend who has always greeted me warmly, no roasting here. Reiley is one gem of a human being, and while we only shared a room for one year in college, I will forever refer to her as my roommate. I can't wait for my future children to meet 'Aunt Reiley,' because it is my full intention for us to be close for the rest of our lives. She is my favorite hug, least surprising contact to show up on my screen, and most frequent choice for road trip driver. The songs that make me think of Reiley include Beyonce's 'Countdown,' Nitty Gritty Dirt Band's 'Fishin' in the Dark,' Lake Street Dive's 'Good Kisser,' and T-Pain's 'Cyclone.' I can always count on Reiley to make me laugh and to be a genuine friend and listener. I'm so excited to share her with you.

Reiley grew up in the sticks of rural North Carolina, in a small town called Locust. Every time she talks to someone from home, she gets some of her twang back in her voice, lest we ever forget her southern charm. Family has always been the biggest priority in Reiley's life, so I've had the pleasure of meeting her parents and three sisters. The only thing I have in common with Reiley's childhood is we were both raised in Christian homes, knowing the Lord for as long as we can remember, which we both count as huge blessings. Reiley illustrates her lifestyle at home as a mixture of performance-driven and grace-based. She always felt love from her parents and God, but she still felt a need to prove her worth, show her strength, and to avoid appearing weak. Despite their closeness as a family unit, she was never truly vulnerable with her family, desiring to please her parents and always keep a smile on her face.

Let's jump forward to Reiley during her junior year in college, while we lived together. Her family had an unfortunate event. After this, our house would gather around Reiley, holding her hand, listening and crying with her.

Eventually Reiley turned to counseling, which helped Reiley to feel emotions even when she was afraid to. Her therapist helped her to process her situation and her emotions in a healthy way. While she found counseling to be valuable, she also found it to be incredibly exhausting emotionally and physically. Sessions would often bring her to tears, and it was never easy.

When we graduated, Reiley moved to Winston Salem, NC for the Fellows Program, which included living with a host family. Moving to a new city she loved, taking a break from counseling, and experiencing daily life with a family who wasn't her own was a huge change of pace. She describes this period in Winston as a chance to take a breath and rest from a tumultuous two years; it was a blessing. Living with her host family was a sweet experience for Reiley, an opportunity to reflect on her own upbringing and to see how another family functioned. She got to take a step back and "live with a family whose problems were different than mine. It was so refreshing."

In March 2020, the world started to shut down while Reiley was still living with her host family. Many others from her program opted to move back home to quarantine with their own families, but Reiley chose to stay with her host family in Winston. Intentionally moving back in with her family in Locust, where she would have to face hard and uncomfortable conversations, did not sound appealing to Reiley at first.

Reiley recognized her coping mechanism at the time was hiding, because "being vulnerable is scary, being emotional is scary" and knew living at home would require her to risk being both vulnerable and emotional with her family. Reiley talked to others for counsel, prayed about it, and ultimately decided to move back home after she had already started a life on her own. It was an act of love. Reiley calls the decision "simultaneously one of the hardest and easiest decisions I've ever had to make in my life. The hardest part was getting over my selfishness." Reiley quarantined with her family for a month before her new lease started up back in Winston-Salem. The month was hard, long, and full of growth. While there, she also took a critical step to restart counseling. She's still in counseling and "having the conversations that needed to be had."

Thinking about the lessons she has learned so far, Reiley now knows vulnerability works differently than she originally thought. Vulnerability isn't about relinquishing control or giving up a part of yourself, it's about letting someone else carry your burden with you. She has learned when seeking vulnerability from others, it only works well when she is vulnerable with them, too. Vulnerability on both sides allows room for hurt to be addressed, processed, and then part of the past. With Reiley's family, being vulnerable is still incredibly challenging. She's still working on that, and each time she's received in love, she's more encouraged to keep going in the future.

While it's generally understood people love to talk about themselves, it is usually only to varying degrees. While I love to tell friends stories about my life, there are certainly topics where I have my walls up! The stories involving my deepest hurts and insecurities, those are much harder to share. Several of the stories I have included in this book are what I would deem my most vulnerable moments. Wherever you are on the scale of openness, there are likely some topics you put up a little resistance before sharing. That can be healthy; I'm not telling you to share your deepest, most vulnerable moments with the person in the elevator who asked how your day was. Not everyone is looking for that level of detail, and not everyone deserves that level of detail. I recommend sharing vulnerable moments with those you trust and those who can help lighten your load, even if it feels bold.

When have you taken a risk to let someone in on how you're really feeling?

6

Dating

Fear of rejection can hold us back from asking someone out or starting a relationship. Sometimes we must work up the nerve, summoning our courage before pushing past that fear. Even if they say yes, it's not necessarily easy from there. In a relationship, there are still risks. Communicating your preferences can create opportunities for disagreements. This can come up in topics like cleanliness, spending habits, or defining the status of your relationship. "Are we exclusive?" "Do you want to move in with me?" "Will you marry me?"

Ending relationships can be even scarier than starting them. Not all breakups are the result of an event, a clear argument, or a mutual decision to move on. Often, we are comfortable and happy enough in relationships, but if you realize it is not the right relationship for you in the long-term, it can be despairing. You still care deeply for them and don't want to cause them pain. So, you can choose to stay in a relationship that mostly works, comfortable in your routine, security, and physical affection. Or you can choose to say goodbye and venture back into the status of being single, having to start over again.

Our choices in romantic relationships directly impact the other person. We don't get the privilege of being the sole party experiencing the consequences. The stakes are higher this way, and it's no surprise several people's boldest moments involved changing their relationship status.

When You Know, You Know

Vince is a ball of energy, and he leads recruiting and everything surrounding the two-year rotational program that kickstarted my career. Vince is loud, smiley, and quick to tell you his wife looks like the actor, Anna Kendrick. He has also been a friendly presence, supporting me as I have made three cross-country moves. He has helped with interview jitters, location preferences, and countless moving logistical questions.

Vince shared a story with me that began when he was in New York, killing it in a previous recruiting job. He was doing so well he had a reputation. One day he picked up the phone to hear, "Hi, this is Meagan, I'm the new member of your team. Listen, I'm gonna shoot you straight. I heard you are the best person on this team, and I want to be better than you." Wow, that sounds bold of her, doesn't it? Yet Vince wasn't the least bit fazed. He set up plans for her to shadow him at upcoming recruiting events.

Here is where the story turns from professional to personal. When they met, they "immediately hit it off… immediate chemistry." Vince thought "this is a really cool person, I'm really excited." As they were prepping for their flight, they got several flight delay notifications. Instead of waiting in the airport, they relocated to talk and wait at a bar. Later, the flight was cancelled, and they kept talking. For eight hours non-stop, they were "talking about life, talking about things, really just connecting in such a unique way." Together they travelled back to New York for a couple days before parting ways back to their own cities.

When they had first met, both Vince and Meagan were in other relationships. In fact, Vince was dating his sister-in-law's best friend. But as the next couple weeks passed, he realized he no longer wanted to be in that relationship, despite its stability. He ended things, making the decision he thought was best for him.

When Vince and Meagan travelled again for work, this time it was a trip throughout the East Coast. The first night they caught up he said, "I just want to let you know, I'm out of the relationship I was in, and I'm interested in spending more time with you." To his surprise, she was no longer in a relationship either. Suddenly both available, they started dating.

They spent the next three weeks travelling for work, spending all their time together and learning about each other quickly. They had deep conversations, created a joint Spotify playlist, and discovered quirks like "she's a weirdo when it comes to food!" Their travels lined up with scheduled family visits, so, very early on, they met the other's parents. Everything in their relationship was happening fast-forward.

After the trip, they were again in their separate cities. She came to visit him in New York, and as they were eating ice cream, she made a bold joke, "wouldn't it be funny if we got engaged?" To this, Vince said, "yeah, that would be hilarious, but we would need a ring first." He took her to a nearby Macy's and they started to look at rings. For Vince, it wasn't a joke at all. In fact, the very next day, he went back to the store on his own. When the associate pulled out the 'perfect ring,' on sale, he bought it right then and there. Only a few days later, he proposed at her hotel.

At this point, Vince and Meagan had only known each other for 2½ months and had been dating less than four weeks. Remember, his friends and family saw him go from dating one girl to proposing to a different one a month later. He learned so much about friendships during this time, some friends being more supportive than others. Looking back, Vince notes, "there were lots of really difficult things that could have stopped me," including lifelong friendships, self-perception, risk it wouldn't work out, and fear he was caught up in emotion. Regardless of all that, he reasoned, "this was worth taking a leap of faith, there wasn't a point in time I felt nervous." So, he wasn't afraid to dive in.

Vince knew he wanted the relationship to go somewhere serious, and when Meagan made the joke, "that was the moment it became a real thing." He didn't think long-distance relationships worked and wanted their relationship to be a reality. "If I was in any other mindset, I wouldn't have taken it seriously." But based on the core of what they had, where they each were individually, and the conversations they had by that point, the timing felt right for them. He says, "It's inconsequential how much time it was, because I knew everything I wanted to know."

Vince didn't feel like he was making an analysis of risk vs. reward when he proposed after a few weeks of dating. For him, he thought the timing was right. He has repeatedly said "when you know, you know," and emphasized it felt like a "no-brainer." Despite his certainty with his choice, he describes it as out of character behavior, "it was bold for me at the time… it wasn't the norm for me, but this person wasn't normal." Vince proved he found Meagan anything but normal, remarkably describing her with the following line, "no matter how hard you want to pull away, the force of that person's soul pulls you in."

They got married a year after their engagement, and it has been six years since then. Vince says he is "a better person every day" because he's with his right person. Vince and Meagan now live in Meagan's childhood hometown, and she motivated him to apply for his current role. In general, he always tries to be open and positive, trusting the good things he sees in his life are in fact, good things. "You have to trust you know it's right." His experience of getting to know Meagan opened him up to recognizing good opportunities when he sees them. He pushes past the "what ifs," because he knows they will always be there.

When have you said yes to a new opportunity? When have you acted without hesitation because it felt right?

Back up Against the Door

Let's rewind to my sophomore year of high school. I was about a month and a half into a relationship with a boy we will call

Derek. He had his driver's license before I did, so most of our dates would end either with him dropping me off, or hugging goodbye at my front door. One night is specifically and clearly implanted in my memory. Neither of us had ever kissed anyone before, and I really wanted him to kiss me that night. But he only hugged me goodbye like normal, and I closed the door behind him as he walked to his car parked on the street. Frustrated, I dramatically leaned my back up against the door, thinking to myself "Augh… I really wanted him to kiss me." I took a deep breath, then opened the front door again. He had opened his car door but paused when he saw me.

Using his full name, I asked him, "when are you planning on kissing me?" To this, he said nothing. He closed his car door and walked straight up to me. When he walked up the steps and was inches away from my face, he whispered, "now!" and kissed me. When he pulled away, he turned our cinematic scene back to reality with a line that to this day still cracks me up, "Yeah, my mom's been asking me the same thing." So smooth. I laughed and we said goodnight once again. This time, when I closed the door behind me, I was ecstatic. After a few brief moments to let it sink in, I ran to the living room where my mom was on the couch reading; I told her everything.

I don't remember an internal assessment of risk; I just remember knowing what I wanted and asking for it. But the risk was there. This was something I had waited for, slightly afraid, because I didn't know what to expect. But in the moment, all I could think about was the reward. My decision process was uncharacteristically speedy. I couldn't spend too long contemplating whether to reopen my door - I only had a few moments until he was gone. Luckily for me, it worked out.

When have you asked for what you wanted?

Derek and I dated for five years in total. That was a quarter of my life at the time. Throughout the entirety of that relationship, I identified as half of a couple, our lives were intertwined around each other. His friends were my friends, and he was my best friend. We were happy and comfortable. I felt safe and loved. So why am I not still dating Derek?

It's challenging to articulate what happened because there wasn't one thing that went wrong. But when I thought about the possibility of marriage with Derek, I wasn't excited. In fact, when friends and adults in my life would ask, only somewhat seriously, if I was thinking about marrying him, I was terrified. But isn't marriage something you should be excited about?

There was likely a combination of things dampening my excitement, my youth and fear of commitment at the forefront. He never put a timeline on our relationship or even explicitly brought up a future marriage between us. Yet, I put a load of pressure on myself. More accurately, I was freaking out. I found myself more comfortable saying "why not?" than finding reasons why I wanted him specifically. So, I prayed over and over that God would give me a desire for Derek, yet nothing changed.

It was excruciating to think what that meant. I cared so much for him, no part of me wanted to hurt Derek. I didn't want to say goodbye. I felt like a monster, because I knew how much pain I was choosing to put him through. I felt incredibly guilty.

I put the breakup off for a couple weeks, not looking forward to it, and hoping I might change my mind after all, but eventually, I couldn't hide it any longer. I asked him to come over and had less than 15 minutes before I had to face my biggest fear. When he arrived, I was already in tears. I gave him as much explanation as I could muster, and apologized repeatedly, hating myself to the core. He left that night and I wept. I felt as though my world was crumbling around me, and I was left holding the Jenga piece that caused it all to fall. I don't know if I got a wink of sleep that night, I was so distraught. I wanted to take it back. I wanted to beg for his forgiveness and ask if he would pretend none of this had ever happened. I had no idea what I was doing, so I did the only thing I could - cry. That first night was the most loss and pain I had experienced at that point. The next day I was exhausted and felt empty.

This timeline left me at the beginning of an uneventful winter break, so I was without distractions I would normally have during school. Overwhelmed with my thoughts, I journaled and prayed, convinced the pain was a sign I made the wrong decision. I knew it was early, but I wanted to return to my happy, normal self. I would plan logistics, like which day I would need to get back together with him in order to watch the next basketball game by his side. But I set a goal to wait at least one week before running back to something I worked up all this courage to leave. I waited a week, fully planning on texting him once my eternity of a time limit was up. To my surprise, once I had gotten several nights of sleep, the need to reunite wasn't as urgent. I had a few friends offering activities as distractions, and the tiniest part of my pain had turned numb. I still wrestled with my thoughts like I had in the preceding month. My journal included a list of all the things I liked about Derek, as I yet again attempted to convince myself I loved him.

Another two weeks passed, much of it spent hiding in my room. In January, we made it back to campus. Finally, I could surround myself with things and activities again, and I was relatively okay. I was even somewhat relieved to spend the time however I chose, without having to fear I was letting someone else down. There were several things I loved to do but didn't because Derek didn't enjoy them or didn't approve of them. I started to learn more about myself and what it meant to be me, when I am the whole, not just a half. Through this, I decided space from Derek would be healthy, because when we spoke, it was nothing short of agony. I was now confident in my decision to break up.

But it wasn't all fixed by any means. Our friends felt like they had to pick sides. Which one of us would they invite? They all knew it would make sense to give us space from each other, but Derek didn't like the idea of space. He took the breakup poorly. While it pained me greatly, his actions and words only confirmed to me I had made the right choice. He would text me hurtful messages at all times of the night, blaming me for every negative emotion he experienced. I still felt guilty for the monster in me who chose to inflict this pain on him, so I never mustered the courage to block him like some ex's do. But those messages always seemed to arrive on my hardest days, and they had sunk deep. If I didn't respond, he would double his efforts, upset I had ignored him. He convinced me to meet him one-on-one, several more times throughout the semester, and one time I heard a loud thud after I closed the door behind me. He had hurled something forcefully at the door, barely missing me, but successfully terrifying me. He wrote me a letter, airing all his grievances with me, but also asking me to take him back. These were the unhealthy, conflicting communications he would send at all hours.

Eventually, I got the space I had been seeking, crystallized by summer internships states apart. For a long time, I was angry with Derek for the ways he lashed out at me while he was in pain. It took two years until I was able to let that anger go. I called and apologized one final time - not for the breakup, but for the anger I felt towards him in the aftermath.

He went from being my entire universe, to being someone I used to know. Crazy. I used to know every mundane detail of his life. I used to excitedly mention his name and tell stories about things from his life or family at the faintest relevance to the conversation. Now, I hesitate even if the topic at hand is screaming relevance to a story that includes him. I have no clue where he is living, what he's doing, or who he is with. From now on, that is how it will continue to be.

No, this isn't your classic happy romance story. It's not only the end of a relationship, but the end of my identity as I knew it then. It was excruciating, but I would also call it bold. I was very aware of the risk I was taking and the pain it would bring. I boldly left my comfort zone, when I could have easily stayed in it so much longer.

What is a challenging decision you have made that didn't immediately present positive results? What's a situation or someone you have chosen to say goodbye to?

Newfound Voice

In relationships, we can learn so much about ourselves, how we want to connect with our significant other, and how to communicate those preferences successfully. My friend, who we'll call Sophie, learned all these things in her first serious relationship. Sophie has been a part of my life for many years now, and I am so incredibly thankful for her. She is a genuine friend and has never judged me - even though she knew me in my cringiest phases growing up. She is inclusive and considerate to a level unmatched by many. We have had an abundance of interests in common, with the two most constant being running and long talks. Ideally, we can do both at the same time, but that depends on how in-shape we are!

When I challenged Sophie to think about her boldness, she opened up a previously closed off experience. Despite all our talks, Sophie hadn't disclosed everything in her life. She hadn't brought up the most uncomfortable things, even though I was one of her closest friends. She felt confused and anxious as she stayed quiet, processing internally. She felt isolated in her struggles yet put on a brave face.

This story, previously unbeknownst to me, reveals how Sophie discovered her voice, learned how to advocate for herself, and express what she needed. Her journey starts in a classic coming of age scenario. Sophie's sophomore year of high school involved exploration of her interests and talents. What did she want to be when she grew up? What food, music, and activities made her happy? What clothes made her feel comfortable and confident? Who did she want to surround herself with? These were all questions she contemplated as she navigated the new school year.

At the beginning of the year, she started dating one of our best guy friends, we will call him Michael. Around this same time, many of the girls started to wear athletic clothes to school. Think oversized t-shirts, Nike running shorts, Nike crew socks, and Sperry boat shoes. Not the best look in hindsight, but we were happy to join in on the comfy trend. After some period of time, Michael asked Sophie why she "never dressed up for him" anymore. He worried her consistent choice of comfortable outfits indicated a lack of interest in him. Sophie did her best to reassure him, but she knew his concern was not resolved when the gifts she received from him on special occasions were exclusively dresses. What he intended as a kind gesture, she perceived as a request to change her habits. In the coming months and eventually years, Sophie was plagued with self-doubt, spending an hour in the morning staring at her closet before feeling defeated, finally selecting something to wear that day. She attempted to factor

Michael into many everyday decisions out of respect, and her hope to please him.

After dating for a while, they took their relationship to a new level. "We decided we were ready for sex," which Sophie found both exciting and scary. As they started to explore this side of their relationship, she found she wasn't always ready or interested when the topic came up. He misinterpreted this as a lack of interest in him rather than hesitancy towards sex in general. At this time, Sophie says she "hadn't learned how to express my emotions," making it challenging to clear things up. Through this, she would sometimes choose to please him instead of making her instinctive decision to slow down or stop.

One Valentine's Day they were in a period of long-distance dating and Michael had a surprise planned for the two of them. He had booked them a night at a local hotel to secure themselves some privacy. When the surprise was revealed, Sophie was immediately uncomfortable with the idea of staying the night, but her mind raced. She loved him and didn't know how to tell him about her discomfort with a night of intimacy. So, she didn't tell him. She was "worried somehow it was my fault, I was in the wrong for not wanting it… I loved him; I didn't want him to feel bad about it." So even though she didn't truly want to, she consented that evening. She caved in to make him happy. The next day when she was home in the safety of her own room, she cried continuously. "It was traumatic." She tried to pick herself back up and pretend everything was fine. She felt she "didn't have many people she could talk to" and bottled her emotions up inside herself. "Every time I hung out with him it was stressful."

Over a break from school, Michael came back into town. Sophie was hoping their relationship would get to a more positive and comfortable place now that they were in a setting that was familiar and safe. She told herself their problems would be eliminated. But one night when things started progressing physically, it hit her. The setting hadn't made anything better. Sophie "was about to cave in again but finally said no… I had been uncertain up until that point. This time I could feel it physically, this is not what I want to do, and I need to be able to voice that." Fortunately, she found her voice and let it all out. The conversation opened a channel of communication exposing other components of their relationship that were unhealthy. With everything out in the open, they eventually agreed to end their relationship.

After the breakup, Sophie and her mom went on a shopping spree for retail therapy. This was the first time in a few years she was able to focus on her personal answer to the earlier question, "What clothes made her feel comfortable and confident?" Let me tell you, she has since found a variety of 'go-to' outfits way more flattering than crew socks and boat shoes, and the great news is they still make her feel comfortable!

When I asked Sophie how she has used her newfound voice since that day, she recalled several examples. One pertains to her interactions with Michael. As Sophie's voice has grown, she has been able to go back and express what she went through even more clearly to Michael. They were able to become friends, and in the years since, Michael has visibly grown in communication and maturity. His relationships are healthier than the one they shared years ago.

Sophie has used her voice in other friendships and relationships. "It took me a while, but I can voice what I want," instead of just giving in to what she thinks someone wants from her. She can be honest and stick up for herself. Overall, she knows, "I'm not afraid, if I do have a strong opinion, to voice it." She can be kind without overthinking or sacrificing her well-being out of fear or hurting someone's feelings. This was a major process of growth for Sophie, and it created future possibilities for her. Now she knows she can speak up, be accepted, and received in love.

When have you broken a cycle of one of your habits? When have you stood up for yourself and your needs, or put in boundaries?

Truth Over Ignorance

Gabby is a kind, inclusive woman. She's got a big, contagious smile and an impressive sense of style. We met during our two-year rotational program at work and have connected further over our shared beliefs. Gabby's chosen bold story encompasses faith and a specific relationship.

Let's call her boyfriend at the time Haribo. When they started dating in college, Gabby "believed in God, but I wasn't an active Christian. I wasn't taking time to develop my relationship with God." Through the course of their relationship, Haribo brought Gabby to his church and kickstarted her personal Bible reading. Previously, Gabby had been interested, but intimidated by the idea of reading the Bible and thinking more intentionally about what she believed. Haribo answered Gabby's questions about his beliefs and patiently encouraged her to prioritize fleshing out her own beliefs. "As I got into it, I realized it wasn't enough to just be a good person." Gabby found this time to be educational and full of growth. She was happy with her relationship and how they interacted, whether in periods of joy or anxiety. "It felt perfect." Their lives became intertwined, and before long, Gabby says she "felt like he was going to be my husband, so I was planning accordingly. Every decision centered around that."

Around two years into dating, Gabby started to identify "different red flags that wouldn't be sustainable for a strong marriage." As they attempted to develop their relationship, they argued on aspects of their beliefs, morals, and values. The "constant conflict was a boiling pot, waiting for something to boil over." One day, when they were coming close to a resolution, Gabby was caught off guard by Haribo announcing he wasn't ready for a relationship. She interpreted this as him wanting to break up, but when she asked him, he said this wasn't the case.

They were doing long-distance at that time, and the next time Gabby visited Haribo, everything seemed to fit back into place. It appeared all his qualms and all their quarrels had disappeared. "We were able to play house so well… We still looked like a couple on track to get married. We went on double dates, events with extended family, church, family dinners, knowing our relationship had an expiration date." After a great day 'playing house' together, Gabby felt a knot start to grow in the pit of her stomach. She noticed herself getting irritated by things that typically wouldn't have bothered her.

When she couldn't ignore it any longer, Gabby left to go to the bathroom and prayed behind closed doors for guidance and discernment. She knew she couldn't keep acting like everything was okay not knowing where her relationship with Haribo stood. When she returned, Gabby directly asked Haribo if he still felt the hesitation he had in their previous conversation. She was hoping he would say no, that he felt good and was ready to dive back into making the relationship work. By asking that specific question, Gabby found her boldness in "choosing truth over ignorance." To her dismay, he said yes, confirming he did want to be single. Gabby remembers responding to Haribo, "based on what you're saying it sounds like we should split up." In that moment, despite her fears being realized in a heart-breaking way, Gabby felt at peace, the knot in her stomach had disappeared.

No breakup from a loved one is easy, but Gabby knew she needed to "step out in faith," despite whatever would come next. She trusted her God was a God of abundance who would prosper her, give her hope and a future, as stated in Jeremiah 29:11. Gabby and Haribo parted on good terms, still caring deeply for each other. She knew "embodying the love I had for him was giving him the space he needed."

When have you confronted a harsh reality? When have you declined an opportunity in anticipation for a greater one in the future?

Despite Hesitation

In the final relationship story, my friend shared a choice she truly regrets making. We'll call her Leah. We met in Charlotte, and in addition to our faith, we have discovered many shared interests. From being active with hiking, line dancing, and volleyball, to staying home with romantic comedies and game nights, we have spent tons of time together. She is a kind friend with whom I really identify, and always feel accepted by. She is genuine and doesn't try to make herself look cool, though I certainly think she is! I have only known her for a few months so far, but I am excited to see what memories we will create together in the future.

Leah and a boy that we'll refer to as Steven became friends in early middle school, seeing each other weekly at youth group. As they grew older and closer, their frequent conversation was filled with banter and competition that was "kind of flirty." So, at one point, Steven "tried to move out of the friend zone." Unfortunately for him, Leah didn't reciprocate his feelings. After a short period of space, they regained their friendship to the point they talked every day. After another year of close friendship, Steven again told Leah he had feelings for her. In a familiar cycle,

Leah did not reciprocate. Also familiar, they took some space before once again resuming their close friendship.

They went to separate schools for college, and this was Leah's first time without an established community. She felt lonely and started to consider if maybe she did have any feelings for Steven. As he was starting to become more mature, she felt like she could see "new sides to him." That first semester, Leah told a mutual friend she might be interested in Steven after all, but "it doesn't matter... I have no interest in starting anything when we're not in the same place physically." She didn't plan to ever tell him, she just wanted to "toy with it in her mind."

Steven and Leah stayed close, visiting each other's schools and seeing each other at home during the holidays. By the end of Leah's sophomore year at college, Steven professed his feelings towards her a third and final time. The outcome was like the times previously, with rejection, space, and an eventual rekindling of their friendship. They were "essentially repeating the same cycle."

After graduation, Leah moved to Charlotte, but when COVID-19 became more serious in the US, she moved back home. Conveniently, Steven returned home as well, resurging Leah's internal questions of possible feelings towards him. One of Leah's closest friends pushed her to tell Steven how she felt. But Leah didn't like or listen to that advice. She didn't really know if she had feelings for Steven, and even if she did, she didn't think it would work out. She avoided Steven for the first couple months they were home, "too nervous to see him." Leah was worried if she spent more time with him one-on-one, she would develop concrete feelings. If she had feelings, their history indicated Steven would reciprocate, and "something could happen." But Leah didn't know if this is what she wanted to happen. So, she consulted her mom, who told her to "see if something was there." Leah spent two full months "all up in my head about it."

Eventually, Leah and Steven made plans for dinner. Going into the night, Leah didn't know if she wanted to tell Steven she had thought about him romantically. She was leaning towards not saying anything because "I don't do anything without a plan." Leah had a strong suspicion if she opened that door to their relationship, "it would change things…we were either going to date and get married or we would be done being friends."

At dinner, they got along well, 'like always.' About an hour into their conversation, the topic turned towards lists of what they look for in significant others. "I can't help but think I check off all or most of the things on his list…and I give him my list and can't help but think he checks off mine." This is the moment where Leah knew she must make a choice. She would either tell him right then or keep her mouth shut forever. "Despite having great hesitation about what my feelings were … I decide I am going to say something."

Leah was bold but didn't proclaim anything stronger than the truth. She simply said she had considered the possibility of them dating. But this was more than Leah had ever indicated before, and Steven was shocked. "He sat in silence for a minute… really taken aback." Eventually his response confirmed her suspicions, that yes, he was interested in her. "At first it was giddy excitement, "oh my gosh, we're going to do this!" She felt good; despite her hesitation, she was confident and gratified in her choice.

After eight years of friendship, Leah and Steven finally started a romantic relationship. They already knew each other closely and Leah described their 'honeymoon phase' as amazing. Unfortunately, their proximity was short-lived because Leah had to move back to Charlotte. But Leah wasn't worried. She expected long-distance to be hard, but they had a plan. Steven had already scheduled a trip to visit her in two weeks and after that, they would take turns visiting each other, playing it by ear. Leah felt good about where they were as she packed up her car. But as she made the 9-hour drive alone, she started to feel very anxious.

Leah moved in and got settled, "genuinely excited for him to come visit." When Steven arrived for the weekend, she switched into her 'hostess mode,' fully focused on ensuring he enjoyed his stay. After he left, she thought through how the weekend went. As she replayed the weekend in her head and re-evaluated how she felt about their relationship, Leah knew she had to break up with him. She broke the news over Facetime, leaving Steven "incredibly blindsided and upset."

Sadly, since their breakup, they haven't communicated at all. Leah has "truly lost him as a friend... I miss talking to him...I miss our friendship." Some days the loss can feel crushing. Unlike the past, there would be no rekindling of friendship following their space apart. Sadly, there was only finality this time.

Reflecting on her decision to tell Steven she was interested in him, Leah doesn't doubt whether it was bold. She says choices require a "special type of boldness when it involves another person," especially their emotions. Perhaps her biggest risk in telling him was she didn't truly know how she felt. Before she told him, part of her knew that even though she was interested, it wouldn't work out. Part of her knew and "that's why I hesitated." In the moment, heeding the advice of people she loved, Leah "pushed past in boldness." She pushed past her natural feeling of concern and hesitation, only to later realize that listening to her initial concerns could have saved them both pain.

Throughout this book, I have emphasized the positive aspects of boldness. Most of the stories in this book showcase positive results, following a high risk, high reward pattern. This story, however, is different. Leah often regrets making this bold decision. As a Christian, Leah believes God brought several good things, like closure, from their short-lived relationship, but it "doesn't mean it was the right choice." She thinks she and Steven could have reached those benefits without sacrificing their relationship. This experience makes her more aware of the words and timing she chooses when communicating with others. "Words are powerful." Leah argues not every feeling needs to be vocalized, because not every feeling needs to be heard. When Leah chose to voice her feelings, knowing deep down they didn't change the relationship for her, Leah opened herself up to the consequences.

When have you ignored your gut-instinct, making a decision that left you with regrets?

7

For Others' Benefit

Many, but not all the stories shared so far were centered around personal decisions. People found boldness answering questions like: What is right for me? What will stretch me and help me grow? What should I do next with my life? Those are all important questions worth asking. In contrast, the upcoming stories bring to light what boldness can look like when you ask questions like: What will protect the people around me? How can I provide safety or security?

Sometimes what we are putting on the line doesn't just impact us as an individual. Sometimes we choose to put ourselves at risk because it will improve the circumstances for someone else. We may risk sacrificing our comfort, pride, job, or something else of value. That is bold if you ask me.

12 Phone Calls

Brendan is a friend to all, and it never surprises me when he strikes up a conversation with a stranger. He gives every human being the same potential to be a new buddy. I met him in precisely that type of scenario when I shared an airport shuttle with him to our first work event. By the time we arrived, another new coworker thought Brendan and I had known each other since we were kids. Today, he's grown to be much more than a friendly coworker who radiates positivity and obscure sports knowledge. He is my handyman, habitual movie night buddy, confidant, and fellow party planner! This man can chug a beer quicker than anyone; he simply deletes them.

Brendan grew up the eldest of four, and proudly talks about his siblings all the time. I had the pleasure of meeting one of his siblings recently and met his dad a few years back. When we interned in Charlotte together, his dad came to visit and took our small band of coworkers out to dinner. Afterwards, his dad pulled me aside and handed me a gift card with a balance large enough for all of us to return for another meal. I said thank you and took it as an opportunity to joke to Brendan that his parents were paying his friends to spend time with him! To Brendan, this kind of generosity fit right into his image of his father.

Shortly before graduation, Brendan learned a series of facts which drastically altered his understanding of his father. He came to find there was deceit in all the truths he expected his dad to uphold. His dad's choices included infidelity in marriage, shaming, and outright lies. To top it all off, he ran a Ponzi scheme business that swallowed the money of their close family members and friends. When the news came out, Brendan's previous image of his dad was shattered: "He's my dad but I will never look at him the same." Brendan questioned many of his positive memories of his father, now realizing what was going on behind the scenes. He experienced a period of shock and hurt, but quickly turned to care for his mom and younger siblings. Only Brendan had the luxury and distraction of not living at home, where anything could be a reminder of the present pain.

When Brendan reflects on the emotional pain his dad caused, he focuses on the irreparable harm his father's actions had on close friends and family. "Imagine stealing $600,000 from your brother, knowing well what it is going towards, trying to pay towards other people's money you lost. It was essentially a Ponzi scheme." The crime earned him spotlights in news articles, placement in rehab, and a potential jail sentence once his court date arrives.

Without the ability to pay back his father's 12 business partners himself, Brendan looked for ways to help, "I'm a doer not a sitter. But I wasn't a grown up and felt limited in what I could do." One idea he had was to call each of the people impacted by his father's choices, apologize on his behalf, and vouch for the innocence of the rest of his family. He didn't want his mom and siblings to lose out on all the relationships and connections they had before. "I was nervous about what their reactions would be. Are they going to take it out on me over the phone? Are they going to double down because they think I sought pity?" After a week of wrestling with his idea, he followed through -- he picked up the phone and called every one of his dad's business partners.

These were people he had known all his life; he'd played sports with their children, spent Christmas Eve or the Fourth of

July with their families, gone on vacations with them, and viewed them as his personal role models. In those conversations, he did several things -- he apologized on behalf of his father, acknowledged the hurt and impact, emphasized his mother and siblings had no part in this scheme and hoped they could find it within themselves to not blame them along with his dad, as he shed tears. This was a very hard conversation for a 21-year-old to have once, let alone 12 times. Their initial reactions brought him relief, saying, "Oh, you don't have to apologize", or "Of course, we would never take it out on any of you." His 'optimistic heart' thought it was progress.

Sadly, as time passed, these promises didn't ring true. Relationships among family and friends devolved into bitter business partnerships. In fact, only one of them is still cordial with Brendan's mom. Some, including a sibling's godmother, simply stopped responding to texts and invitations from Brendan and his siblings. Over two years have passed since Brendan's uncle last talked to them. Other aggrieved partners took his mom to court or approached her angrily in public. After one public interaction where Brendan's mom was badgered for answers she didn't have, Brendan boldly called out the aggressor, identifying their failed promises to keep their anger separate from the rest of the family. Brendan is not typically one for confrontation, but he was fed up and couldn't stop himself from standing up for his mom. He was frustrated that his boldness and efforts in the initial conversations didn't resolve the hurt for the business partners nor prevent tension towards his mom. To this day, he remains angry and disappointed about it, saying, "These people are cut out of my life because of what my dad did." He hopes his dad is convicted, so the people he hurt can have closure.

With this anger, Brendan also feels guilty. He benefited from his dad's theft and seemingly generous lifestyle, living with privileges and opportunities many people will never experience. For example, he feels guilty that, unlike his siblings, he was able to attend the college of his choice, without having to take out student loans. He does his best to funnel his anger and guilt into actions that matter, actions that remediate the current situation. In an attempt to patch things up, he moved to Chicago, where some of his family lives. Starting in 2019, he was a "21-year-old kid trying to right the wrongs of a 52-year-old man. It shouldn't have to fall on me, but for some reason I felt like it did." Now he is a couple years older, and is still wearing this burden, regardless of if it's fair.

I hate this situation for Brendan and his family. I hate that those closest to us can hurt us the most, and his dad took the opportunity to wreak havoc on their lives, all in the name of greed. I hate this had to be a part of Brendan's story, but Brendan didn't share this story hoping to get my pity, or yours. He is a better man because of it… "Yeah, it's not great… every family has their problems. You learn from it, grow from it." His situation created the context for him to step up and be bold. Through many tough conversations, he left his comfort zone, acknowledged the gravity of what his dad had done, and asked for mercy. That took some huge guts.

When have you stopped playing the victim card long enough to act and attempt to resolve your situation? When have you stood up for someone you love?

Confronting Pride

Brendan's story involved apologizing on behalf of his father, but apologizing and acknowledging pain can be challenging, even when you are the one who messed up. Our deeds may be blaringly hurtful, but admitting so out loud may not be our first inclination.

Early in my sophomore year of college, I was introduced to a formerly homeschooled Liv. Little did I know Liv would turn into one of my best friends in the world. I have never met anyone like her. Few people surpass me in energy, but she most certainly does. I remember hearing her loudly run up the steps of our college house for two years, and I would stand up to greet her. I always attempted to be more excited about her arrival than she was, but without fail, she would one-up my enthusiasm.

When the two of us are together, we push each second of the day to its max, making memories and going to bed exhausted. Life with Liv as my best friend has been incredibly eventful and entertaining, but equally as real. Sure, she's the life of the party, but she also thrives on the one-on-one aspect of a relationship. This girl thinks deeper than anyone I've met, and she asks questions with genuine interest. She wants to hear my thoughts on everything from Christian theology, goals, current events, boys, or shoes. We have supported each other throughout hard times in our lives and called each other out for less than stellar choices.

When I think of moments where I have seen boldness in Liv, or some great stories she has shared with me, there are plenty that are eventful. In 2020 alone, she bought a sailboat without any nautical knowledge, survived an intense bear encounter, backpacked in Sequoia National Park with me with minimal prep, and moved to DC!

In case I piqued your interest with the bear encounter, I'll summarize. She was camping with her mom and stepdad, Ray, in the Blue Ridge Mountains. Liv was sleeping in her own tent until she woke up to feeling something heavy on her left leg. She tried to kick it off, and it didn't move. She kicked again, harder this time. The weight disappeared from her leg, but then her tent collapsed around her. She lay there in a moment of fear and yelled out "RAY!" Ray had taken Tylenol PM and didn't respond to her first call. After what felt like an eternity, he met her outside her tent in the darkness. As she was trying to explain what happened, they saw two beady eyes glinting nearby. Afraid, they ran into the remaining tent, and waited silently. Her mom was waking up by now and asking for an explanation, to which Liv quickly shushed her. After a couple eerily quiet minutes, they discovered the bear was still outside. They tried to make loud noises to scare it off, but soon heard it tearing Liv's sleeping pad apart in her crumpled tent.

After some arguments about what to do next, they made their way out of the tent and down the path to a cabin they knew was somewhat nearby. Ray and Liv picked up large rocks on the way to use as weapons and started speed-walking. Liv tried her best to stay calm while telling her mom to pick up the pace and saw those two eyes following them at an uncomfortable distance. They finally reached the cabin and banged on the door desperately, praying someone would answer. Two guys groggily came to the door in their boxers and let them inside. By the time they closed the door behind them, the bear had made it down the steps approaching the cabin door. Safely inside, they set up camp on the cabin floor, and unsurprisingly, Liv didn't sleep a wink that night. When they returned to the campsite the next morning, more of their gear had been destroyed by the bear, so they packed up and drove home. I heard the story over FaceTime the next day during an intense 20-minute lunch break. YIKES!

While I could use this story to describe an example of boldness in Liv's life, she provided a more emotional and relational example. She decided to share a story of a time where she could be construed as the villain and trusted me to tell the story in an honest way. I will begin with much more context than I have in other stories, but stay with me, it's relevant.

When I met Liv, she was meeting plenty of other friends as well. She joined an ultimate frisbee team called Pleiades where one teammate, who we will name Jen, immediately stood out to her as a close and quality friend. Jen was a kind, high energy girl who asked good questions and worked hard to make Liv feel included in her circle. Soon, Jen and Liv were seen everywhere together, often showing up to various activities in a blur, either barefoot, or wearing their matching Chaco's; laughing as they challenged each other to anything and everything. For a couple months the following summer, Liv moved into Jen's family home with her, providing companionship while Jen's parents traveled, taking an opportunity to live rent-free for as long as possible. There were a couple times where I would join them to dance while attempting a kabob recipe with bacon and pineapples, cut each other's hair to save money, or toss a frisbee to master a new throw.

One night when Liv was living with Jen, they had a little too much to drink. Along with their vision, the lines of their friendship got a little blurry. In a very surprising twist for Liv, they hooked up. She didn't really feel that way about Jen but found it fascinating and fun. Who doesn't want to be wanted? Finding out Jen desired her more than she thought was a pleasurable surprise.

Eventually, hooking up became an activity where she started to disregard Jen as an individual, thinking only of what she could get from her. Liv started to become confused about what she wanted. She was "madly conflicted to a tortuous degree," because she savored the attention, but no longer wanted it from Jen. Her troublesome scenario escalated when they moved into the same room of our house, that fall. No longer on their own, their relationship had the potential to be exposed to the rest of our housemates. Liv felt embarrassed, angry, and hurt by what she was doing with Jen. After a week in our college house, she had a conversation with Jen, announcing she wanted to stop. Oof... that conversation must have taken courage.

It wasn't just one awkward and painful conversation, because they shared a room for the rest of the year. To Liv, Jen was an ever-present reminder of a decision she was embarrassed by. She dreaded being around her, and grew increasingly irritable, angry, and even nauseous in her presence. Let me tell you, Liv does not hide her anger well. Just like when she is losing in a card game, I can tell very quickly when she's unhappy. One of the giveaway signs was she stopped acknowledging Jen altogether. She wouldn't make eye contact with her in the house or on the frisbee field. With this act, she demoted Jen to less than human. She refused to respect her and would frequently display her irritation in front of me. Not knowing how to respond to this dynamic, I am sad to admit I stopped inviting Jen to events I knew Liv would be attending.

Jen became a rare sight at our house, coming home late at night and leaving again before I woke up. Occasionally when I would run into her one-on-one, I would see the sweet, fun Jen I had known. We agreed we were overdue for quality time, but then never actually followed up on it. Jen likely felt ostracized in our house, initially meeting all of us through Liv, and was now feeling like she wasn't wanted. Finally, I started to stand up for Jen. When I noticed Liv treated her in a cruel or disrespectful way, I would call her out on it, but the dynamic continued for the rest of my senior year. Looking back, Liv admits, "I was just nasty; I was really mean to her. I worked hard so she wouldn't feel like we had the same friends. I was content to be savagely mean." At the time, she recognized her actions as problematic, but also saw them as unavoidable. She never wanted to be an angry person, but she saw no readily available alternative to dispose of her anger and shame.

That year, Liv started Christian counseling for some other things going on in her life and found an opportunity to be honest about her situation with Jen as well. One emotional session, Liv remembers hearing the words, "God is after your soul, Olivia, not just your situation." That made her slam the breaks. This identity reevaluation came right before a confrontation. In late spring, their ultimate frisbee team traveled to nationals in Wisconsin. One of the nights there, Liv felt cornered by Jen, who was drunk, crying and calling Liv out for how badly she had treated her ex-best friend. Liv was certainly uncomfortable and didn't know how to respond with anything but the silence she had dished out in the months prior.

Several months later, Liv felt "the Lord put on my heart to call Jen and apologize, to acknowledge what I had done." At this point, Liv didn't want to apologize, didn't feel ready to, but the nudge was there. It was now 1½ years since this all started. I had graduated and moved to Chicago, and I learned about all the following events over the phone. When the nudging could no longer be ignored, Liv called Jen and left a voicemail. Her message admitted her wrongdoing and the pain it caused. This was bold. When is the last time you sincerely apologized to someone, or someone else has apologized to you? It is a sad realization, but a genuine apology is a radical occurrence, particularly in today's culture.

She had nothing to gain from this voicemail. Who knows if it would relieve any of her guilt? She wasn't interested in restoring their relationship, just in admitting her bad behavior. For many young hard workers like Liv, life is a constant search to prove one's achievement, and it can be excruciating to think about failures or character flaws. Knowing it is the right thing to do doesn't always make it any easier. This would be the first time she apologized to someone outside her immediate family.

Jen texted her back, asking to meet in a public place. Liv agreed, and their emotions were on display for all the campus to see. Liv was clear she wasn't asking for a reunion of friendship, but she wanted to be specific in her apology. Liv acknowledged her actions led to the loss of friendships for Jen, including mine. She admitted she treated Jen as less than human, disrespecting Jen to serve herself. She owned up to being both unkind and wrong, and only recognizing it because friends like Reiley and I stood up for Jen. Finally, she asked for Jen's forgiveness. To all of this, Jen wept. In this moment, Liv's consequences became visible to her in a dreadfully exposing way.

When describing the situation, Liv says, "To be honest, I can't remember if she forgave me, the conversation was just so incredibly heavy." So, if Liv's apology didn't make them friends again, and didn't even result in forgiveness, what was the point? Did anything change going forward? Yes, and almost immediately at that. Following the conversation, Jen called me. She thanked me for defending her and fighting for her even when she didn't know it was happening. She told me how it comforted her to know she hadn't truly been alone in this battle, because Reiley and I were telling Liv her actions weren't acceptable. Reiley got one of these thank you calls as well, and when Liv heard about them, the point hit closer to home. Hearing someone had to be defended from her and her wrath, she saw that her pride and her sin had been glaring.

Liv never thought someone would need protection from her, and this sparked another round of apologies. She apologized to friends and teammates for the division she had created and for exposing them to her sin, even if it hadn't been directed towards them. As the only Christian on her team, she recognized she hadn't been a great witness of God's love in that season.

Today, Liv consistently extends sincere apologies, making her unique from my other friends. They aren't needed often, but when she realizes she has hurt me in some way, she will not only own up to it, but then ask for my forgiveness. I don't know anyone else who uses the direct phrase, "Will you forgive me?" In the rare circumstance I'm considerate enough to extend an apology to someone, I likely opt not to ask for forgiveness. I either assume I know the answer, or it would be rude, depending on the scenario. But Liv boldly chooses to ask for forgiveness in each of her apologies. She finds that part transformative, because it forces her to humble herself and opens the door for the other person to respond however they choose. Submitting herself to the verdict of the person she has hurt is one way she can restore dignity to them. She understands she is not owed forgiveness and isn't surprised when it is denied from her.

Again, I am faced with a stark difference from fiction. Stories have a connotation of happy endings, but in real life, sometimes we're not granted them. Sometimes, it's just as painful as it was before. Liv's story is a long one and a bold one. I will keep repeating myself until my face turns blue, but bold looks different for everyone. That is why context is crucial. Certain moments become significant or pivotal in our lives, not because it is the only time we have completed that specific action, but because of when and how that action lined up with the rest of our story.

While sincere apologies are a uniquely infrequent occurrence in the culture of a college campus, the boldness was not in the uniqueness. The boldness was in the confrontation with her own pride in a way that could have lost her relationships with her teammates and her housemates. Bringing up what she considered to be the worst of herself, and honestly sharing that with someone whose respect she craved, was brave. Sharing with someone who she had refused to respect for over a year was bold.

When have you acknowledged your wrongdoing?

Sharing in Sadness

Liv has learned so much from her mom, Ms. Carla. Most of my relationship with Ms. Carla has been indirect, hearing about one another through conversations with Liv. I have heard many examples of how Ms. Carla encourages Liv to think wisely and how her passionate faith is shown through every bit of her life. Ms. Carla recently decided to continue her education, picking up counseling courses. She often shares the lessons from these courses with Liv, who in turn, shares them with me. To my delight, I am getting to spend increasingly more time with Ms. Carla, instead of just hearing about her. I'm thankful for the opportunity to share her story.

Ms. Carla was spending a weekend in Delaware with family when she heard news about a dear friend of hers from church. This friend's husband tragically passed away one afternoon while mowing the lawn. The traumatic scene unfolded with paramedics attempting to revive him on the front lawn, while their three children watched with horror through the living room window. The lives of this family were heartbreakingly altered forever. Losing a husband and father all in one, their family would never be the same again.

While many of us are pained to hear this experience and like to think we would offer ourselves as support to a friend in need at such a time, we might hesitate. We might hesitate, because we don't know how to help. We might hesitate, because we don't know what to say, or because we don't want to interrupt or somehow become an additional burden. We might hesitate, because if we went to visit our hurting friend or pick up the phone, it would be uncomfortable, and we wouldn't know what to say. We might hesitate to share in the grief, especially because there couldn't be an expectation of resolution at the end of the first conversation.

However, Ms. Carla did not hesitate. She called her friend because she knew. She knew that pain all too well because she too had experienced a tragic loss. Ms. Carla and her three children were in a similar position after their father, Ms. Carla's husband, passed away unexpectedly several years prior. So, at this moment, Ms.

Carla took on the risk of discomfort and a deeply painful conversation and called her friend. She shared in her sadness and loved her, as she is called to love others through her faith.

Ms. Carla found freedom knowing nothing she could say in that moment could bring her friend comfort or relief. It was freeing because she didn't agonize over the perfect words to say. That first phone call was hard, but Ms. Carla didn't stop there. She called her friend regularly, offering an ear to listen or providing support with things like finances, car maintenance, and childcare. These two families are still a major part of each other's lives, united not only by shared experience, but also love, time, and growth.

I knew of Ms. Carla's personal grief through my friendship and conversations with Liv, but I am honored to hear about it from Ms. Carla's perspective. I am blown away by her willingness to reopen her own deep sense of loss. She isn't defined by her loss and has come to use her experience in a way to help others. Sharing a tragic experience like hers is just one more example of how I recognize boldness in her.

As with many of these bold stories, Ms. Carla's is not just about boldness. The boldness is intertwined with love, grief, and faith. Boldness does not have to act on its own. Boldness can be wrapped up in the human experience in ways where it appears hidden. When looking back at significant moments in your life, they may not feel overwhelmingly bold. When you peel back the layers, where do you see boldness in your story?

Defying Her Manager

I have an incredibly caring and loyal friend, who I'll refer to as Claire, who loves with a passion. This applies to her family, friends, the sitcom FRIENDS, and baking. The first memory I have of her was our freshman year of college when she grabbed her boyfriend's hand and pulled him onto the Davie Poplar bench. Legend has it if you kiss a loved one on the Davie Poplar bench, you will marry them. Not knowing them, I thought it was incredibly bold of her. Once I got to know them as a couple, there was no doubt in anyone's mind they would end up together, bench kiss or not. In 2019, they became the first of our friends to get married.

Before Claire decided which example of boldness to share with me, I tried to help her ideate. There are several moments where I've witnessed her stand up for people she loved, whether it was her younger sister or her husband. But when I brought those examples up, Claire quickly explained while those moments may have appeared bold to me, they did not feel risky for her. It felt riskier to leave the ones she loved without someone to stand up for them. Claire found another example that made the perception of boldness relevant in a different way. What if someone wants you to be 'bold,' but you know their preferred choice isn't right?

When Claire arrived on her sixth day at her current nursing job, her manager asked her to "step up for the team." Phrased differently, they wanted her to boldly leave her comfort zone and test her abilities. The problem was stepping up would entail working alone. At that point, only one third of her necessary training was completed. Working without the guidance of her preceptor would make Claire responsible for the lives of two infants in the Neonatal Intensive Care Unit. To add even more pressure to this scenario, this unit was Claire's dream job. She had been hoping and looking forward to the opportunity to work at this precise hospital, in this precise unit. Now she faced a quandary. Should she defy her manager or defy her comfort zone and the potential safety of her patients?

While it looked differently than her manager hoped, Claire chose boldness that night. She chose to refuse her assignment, viewing her manager's vision of "stepping up" as more reckless than bold. She stood up for herself and advocated that her patients needed more experienced care than she could provide at that time on her own. She put her job, which she had so longed for, on the line. Despite her manager's initial frustration, they made it work. Assignments were shifted around so all patients would be cared for, and Claire would continue her training by working hand in hand with her preceptor. In a follow-up conversation with her manager, she confirmed there was no unresolved tension, and her position was still safe. Phew. In the aftermath, Claire is affirmed the bold call - to say no - was worth the risk.

Sometimes, going solo, trying something new, or "stepping up" may not be the right choice. It may be harmful to you and others. Only you can know when you are ready to take your next leap. When have you said no in order to protect something valuable to you?

The decision is not often between "be bold" or "regret not being bold." Sometimes we keep life going by choosing comfort, safety, financial savvy, routines, and practicality. Many times, we should. Claire showed me that sometimes, choosing those things can be bold, depending on the circumstances. Is making the bold choice always the right choice? No. Not every decision can be bold and that is ok. My whole goal of telling these stories is to encourage bold choices, but only when they are appropriate. Choosing boldness simply for the sake of appearing bold could be the wrong choice, especially if you find yourself in a scenario similar to Claire. I encourage you to decipher whether your option is truly bold, or if it is reckless or naive instead.

8

Takeaways

My friends and family have utterly blown me away through the sharing of their stories. Some of these experiences I knew of beforehand, but even in these, I likely didn't understand the depth of what they were going through until they shared it with me. Some of these stories, as in Chapter 5, directly discuss the risks involved with being vulnerable. Everyone in this book has willingly accepted that risk to share something real with me and now with you. Recognizing the emotions my friends illuminated in their own stories forced me to uncover the pain and fear that hid in the first drafts of my own examples. What you have left is the truth, the full experiences, positive or negative, that come up when people choose to be bold. It is not easy, and we can't always predict how it will turn out. But our lives are more worthwhile because of those bold choices.

Why do bold choices make our lives more worthwhile? It is not because it makes us appear more exciting, or because it gives us better stories to tell, even though this may very well be the case. It's because each time we leave our comfort zone, we find ourselves in an opportunity for growth. This growth can shape us into people who seize the day, meet new people, mend relationships, and more. For me, this growth can help me follow Jesus, the radical man I hope to imitate. My guess is your role model and inspiration didn't get to where they were by staying in their comfort zone, so why should you?

In school, students would make fun of the 'try-hards,' whether they tried hard in studies, sports, or other extra-curriculars. It was cool to excel in these things of course, but only if you didn't have to try hard to do so. The ideal was to coast by with minimal effort and minimal emotional attachment. But if everything is easy and lacks emotion, it sounds boring to me, not cool. If we boldly challenge ourselves, we will certainly fail more often and feel more negative emotions, but we will likely live a more fulfilled life instead of watching from the sidelines.

Being comfortable is not a bad thing on its own, only when it limits you from your potential. Finding comfort and faith in some components of our lives can help us to be bold in others. When I first moved to Charlotte, North Carolina, it was like a breath of fresh air. It felt easy and natural to be in my home state. I moved with a community of 12 coworkers who are more accurately described as friends, along with several others I knew well from high school and college. I was familiar with the subculture of the city and felt like I clicked well with every new person I met. I was confident in my faith and in my job security through work. All these factors made me feel comfortable and safe.

The comfort I felt in Charlotte allowed me to confidently take risks elsewhere. I tried new hobbies, like trapeze and silks. I threw myself into a book without writing experience outside school essays. I told friends how I was really feeling. I ran a marathon with only seven weeks training and no official course, which turned out to be brutal on all accounts, but I did finish!

Most notably, this sense of comfort in several areas of my life helped me to take the first step towards my biggest fear and risk: commitment. I chose and committed to a church, officially joining as a member and began to serve. I chose to stay and commit to the city of Charlotte and the people I met there. I don't know how long I will stay, but it has already been a calendar year, which sets my personal record. So yes, my decision to live in my home state, not far from my family, may sound predictable. It may seem easy or boring. But this is the thing about boldness, you can't always see it from the outside. Boldness is such a personal process; you can only recognize it when you know what an individual feels afraid of or uneasy about.

Someone like me may not blink an eye about the risk of having to establish a new community in a new city. I feel comfortable bouncing around from city to city because it gives me a sense of adventure and lets me explore all my options instead of making a commitment. But this is me, someone who is almost solely motivated by the fear of missing out. By embracing this fear of commitment and the possibility of missing out on what another city might have to offer me, I am able to fully take advantage of what is here for me now in this city. That excites me, terrifies me, and liberates me all at once. For you, the bold decision might be to pack up and move, but that is for you to decide.

After a year of interviewing and talking about boldness, there are a few things I have learned. Here are some takeaways:

Context is crucial.

Different experiences impact whether something is perceived risky for individuals. Timing and current scenarios impact that perception. For example, recent negative experiences like being hurt by a loved one may make it riskier to trust someone again or to open up emotionally. Recent positive experiences like seeing the success of a previous choice, or confidence of reaching a previous goal, may inspire or motivate you to take the next challenging opportunity. A choice can be bold regardless of whether you have made that choice before, especially if the context has changed.

Boldness can come into any area of your life.

Some decisions will involve larger moments of transition or of things more meaningful to you. Other choices may happen when you feel stability and predictability in your life. Many of the examples in this book were chosen due to the impact they had, or because transitions might be the easiest places to remember or identify boldness. But boldness can come through in small, everyday choices.

Sometimes we fail.

When boldness requires effort, we worry that a failure will mean all that effort was for nothing. But if boldness brings you an answer more quickly than waiting around in your comfort zone, it's not for nothing. That effort and discomfort saved you time.

The impact can be unpredictable.

Sometimes you may never recognize the boldness or the weight of a particular choice. Beyond immediate consequences of boldness, I wish I could say one choice is all it takes to change your decision-making process going forward. I wish I could claim everyone who makes a bold choice sees positive success and it would forever change their lives onto a path of further boldness. But there are no guarantees. It is 100% up to you.

So, this is it, I guess. I have completed 30 interviews and shared several examples from my life. My intent with each story included was to bring a fuller picture of boldness before you. I hope these stories sparked memories of boldness in your own life, and that identifying those times in your life empowers you.

I hope that within reason, you will embrace risks within the context of your own everyday choices. As shown through the examples in this book, your choices each day can expand your comfort zone over time, bringing you growth that is hard to earn otherwise. You CAN make bold choices going forward, but are you willing?

I encourage you to ask your friends and family to share stories of their boldness and ask them deep, soul searching questions. You might be surprised with what they share. When you are asked, share your stories in return! **What is your bold story?**

Acknowledgements

This book was clearly a team effort. I couldn't have written this book without the many friends and family members who shared their stories. Thank you, thank you, thank you, for letting me into some of the biggest moments of your lives and allowing me to capture them in Solo Dancing. You inspire me. Thank you for being a part of this and for sharing my enthusiasm for boldness.

Special thanks to James Tatter, Matt Queen, Christine Grotheer, and Catherine Miley for their feedback and edits along the way. Thank you for your encouragements and critiques, I needed them both. Thank you also to my editor, Martin Foner.

Made in the USA
Middletown, DE
11 March 2022